WELCOME HOME

Good News to Prodigals and Elder Brothers

KEN M. BLUE

MEDIA.COM

Welcome Home

Copyright © 2021 by Ken Blue

The views and opinions expressed in this book are those of the author and do not necessarily reflect the official policy or position of Illumify Media Global.

Published by
Illumify Media Global
www.IllumifyMedia.com
"Let's bring your book to life!"

Library of Congress Control Number: 2021916810

Paperback ISBN: 978-1-955043-33-5

Typeset by Jen Clark
Cover design by Debbie Lewis

Printed in the United States of America

Contents

Acknowledgments

Thanks to my wife, Patti, who transformed my longhand into print.

Thanks also to my daughter, Haven Madson, Wayland Blue, and friend Grace Barlow for help with editing.

A special thank you to my son, Emmet, whose theological insight and writing skill improved this book.

Many friends encouraged my efforts, including Kevin and Jackie Freiberg, Doug Wall, Paul Young, Baxter Kruger, Terry Winters, Terry Wardle, and Barb and Jim Shanley.

I needed help and I received it.

Introduction

THE BIG QUESTIONS

Where did we come from? Why are we here? What should we do? If life has meaning, what is it?

Science and technology have answered many important questions. Over the past two hundred years, our life expectancy has doubled, and we now live more pleasant and comfortable lives. We owe this staggering improvement to modern science and technology.

These disciplines deal with facts and not values. They do not, and cannot, answer the big questions we opened with. When asked what caused the universe, their answer is, "Well . . . something."

If there are answers to the big questions, they must be revealed. I, along with a third of the world's population, believe the answers are revealed in the Bible, and most specifically in the revelation of Jesus from Nazareth. In the following pages, I reflect on what Jesus said about the big questions and the implications of his answers.

Before discussing Jesus' teaching, I start in chapter one with observations about the power and pull of family and home. I do so because the importance of family and home are central to what follows. In chapters two through four, we study what Jesus says about God and us in his so-called parable of the prodigal son. There, Jesus reveals the best news ever. In chapters five and six, we consider some of the theological theories and church practices that undermine the best news ever. In chapter seven, I recount how Jesus and the early church changed the world for the better. I also offer ideas on how we, as followers of Jesus, may keep those changes on track. Chapter eight ends where we began, thinking of home.

ONE

Welcome Home

OUR BEST AND worst experiences are in our homes and with our families. If our home is peaceful and loving, it provides us with the best environment. Thomas Jefferson said, "The happiest moments of my life are those I spent in the bosom of my family." If, however, our homes are riven with strife and bitterness, or a spouse betrays us, or a child is seriously ill or in trouble, home can be a form of hell.

I was raised in a broken and unhappy family. It negatively affected me at the time, and still gets the better of me every now and again. Over the past fifty years, my wife and I have formed a large and happy family. Six of my eight children married well and are producing grandchildren at a rapid rate. We all love God and love each other, and when they return home, I echo Jefferson in saying the happiest moments of my life are those spent in the bosom of my family. It's as close to heaven as I will experience on this earth.

I had a close to heavenly experience last Father's Day. It came as a surprise to me. Friends in Australia secretly flew my eight children, along with all my grandchildren, to my home in San Diego. Coordinating their travel from various countries around the world must have been challenging, not to mention expensive. Around noon, I was watching sports on TV. My wife, Patti, excitedly called from outside, so I came quickly. All my children and grandchildren ran up the driveway. The combination of shock and joy sent me to my knees. While we all hugged, laughed, and wept, I yelled out, "If I don't have a heart attack today, then I'm good for another twenty years!" My family was reunited under my roof—my home. It was the happiest day of my life. It was a taste of heaven.

I experience the pull and power of home when I am away from it. Over the past fifty years, I've traveled overseas numerous times, conducting missions, teaching at conferences, and leading business seminars. Many places I visited were exotic, and some were thrillingly dangerous. The people I worked with were glad I came. That said, I never wanted to stay a day longer than I had to. I always wanted to go back home.

Home is where I get off the treadmill of doing more and trying harder to prove my worth. Home is where worth is given—unconditionally.

It appears to me that the powerful pull of family and home I experience is universal. Walking down the streets of large Chinese cities, I saw its citizens dressed drably, walking with heads down, avoiding eye contact. I also attended their wedding celebrations and family reunions. The same people I saw on the streets were transformed. They sang lustily, danced, and hugged. They were home and fully alive.

During the Lunar New Year celebration (also known as the Chinese New Year), the Chinese have the largest human migration in history. Over a billion long-distance journeys are undertaken from cities to homes in the countryside. They do this in order to celebrate with their families and unite in joy and celebration.

The importance of family is seen in what we will do for one another. Parents spend all they have to afford the best medical care for a sick child. Poor, uneducated migrants move to America, work two or three menial jobs to provide for their families and to give their children an education. They live in sacrificial drudgery so their children can have it better.

These examples of what parents will do for their kids are heroic and understandable. However, what other parents do for their offspring is bewildering. Numerous rich celebrities were recently arrested, tried, and convicted for gaming the admission process to universities so their children could attend.[1] They bribed coaches and administrators and paid to have their children's SAT scores fixed. Some spent half a million dollars in this effort. They are now convicted felons and will suffer humiliation for the rest of their lives. They risked it all for their children.

Along the same line, many politicians, including secretaries of state and a vice president, used their power to make corrupt deals with corporations, foreign and domestic, to ensure their already-wealthy children have even more. For them, public service is a way of enriching bloodlines. Investigative reporters who live to expose such malfeasance have done so. Any claim to integrity for the politicians is now gone forever. In a nutshell, we tend to do things for our families we would never do for others.

In the past, I worked for family-owned businesses as a consultant. I was sometimes called because the company's owner would not deal sensibly with a son or daughter involved in the business. The child's incompetence or disruptive behavior would not have been tolerated in another employee. Yet, the owner allowed the morale of his workers and the productivity of his company to suffer. Pragmatism be damned. Kids are (seemingly) more important than a business's bottom line.

I have witnessed other strange things over the years regarding the pull and power of family and home. I know many people, mostly women, who were raised in abusive families, yet they remain totally attached to them years later. Now married with families of their own, they continue to engage with their families of origin, hoping for the change that never comes.

This all seems crazy to me, but that makes me crazy too. I mentioned earlier that I grew up in a broken family. My father abandoned my mom and his three children. I was the oldest, and he left when I was nine years old. I ended up leaving home at age sixteen; thereafter, I had little contact with my mother and siblings. We were not close over the years and had little involvement with each other.

Thirty years after I left home, I was married and raising my own children. By then, my siblings had married and divorced. That's when my mom phoned to ask for help. My brother, mother, and my sister, with her two children, needed a home. She boldly asked if I would buy them a house. I was the sole provider for a wife and eight children, and certainly not wealthy. I hardly knew these people anymore. Inexplicitly, though, I complied. I bought them a house, which became a twenty-year nightmare. When repairs were needed, I paid for them. With the information on the checks I sent, my brother and a computer-savvy friend electronically embezzled thousands of dollars from my bank accounts. When the crime came to light, the FBI said I must press charges. I chose not to. Why? Because I share genes and the same last name with these people, I was impelled to do something irrational and stupid, such as let them off the hook for a crime. Why do family and home exercise such power and pull?

Evolutionists offer theories. They speculate that our attachment to family is a remnant of our evolutionary past. They suggest that kin groups who defended and took care of each other were more likely to survive and pass on their genes. There may be something to that, but from what I witness, that theory is too shallow. There is way more than that going on, as we have seen.

I have concluded that there is a more plausible explanation. I think we are hardwired for family and home because of who made us and why. The Bible, the teaching of the early Church Fathers, and the ancient creeds say that the Creator is a family—Father, Son, and Spirit. This first well-adjusted family created us in its image. The three persons of the Trinity think, feel, and act as one. The one God is relational and created us for relationship. Our deepest needs are met in connection with others, especially family members. We long for a good home because we came from one.

The idea of Father, Son, and Spirit as family becomes less abstract as we follow Jesus during the three years of His recorded history. As we see, He was close to His Father. He often rose early to pray and spend time with Him. The Spirit came to His aid during His temptation in the wilderness (Matthew 4).

In Matthew 3:16–17, we witness a kind of family reunion. When Jesus was baptized by John, He came up out of the water, "And lo, the heavens were opened unto Him, and He saw the Spirit of God descending like a dove and lighting upon Him. And lo, a voice came from Heaven, saying, 'THIS IS MY BELOVED SON IN WHOM I AM WELL PLEASED'" (TMB).

The Father and Spirit unite with the Son at the Jordan River. Their physical and audible presence affirmed and strengthened Him for his mission to rescue us and bring us home. It would cost Him his life, but bring us home He did.

Paul explained, "Long before God laid down the earth's foundations, he had us in mind, had settled on us as the focus of his love. Long ago he decided to adopt us into his family through Jesus Christ (Ephesians 1:3–6). God created us in his image. "Male and female he created them (Genesis 1:27)." Shortly after, we went astray and hid from our Creator. Naked and vulnerable, we feared judgment (Genesis 3). We kept hiding until Jesus came to reveal the true nature of His Father and to show us that it's safe to come out of hiding and return home. And, whether we know it or not, we are already home by adoption through Christ.

Knowing and believing this makes all the difference. If we know who we are and whose we are, concern about our worth subdues. Anxiety regarding God's disapproval of us is transformed into trust and affection. If we believe that Jesus did everything that needed doing and we are safe home, we will not perform for approval. Been there. Done that. Got the T-shirt. Wrote the review. I am finally past needing approval.

This, in turn, makes us more patient, caring, and generous toward others. As a result, we are happier, and so is everyone else. One person so transformed nudges the world a little toward the kingdom of God and away from hell. Sensing the security of a loving home will do that.

I have attempted, thus far, to say that the powerful pull of family and home is because of who made us and why. This answers the first big question. We are hardwired for family because we came from one. If we have a good family and home here on earth, we have a taste of this unseen reality in heaven. If not, we know the pain of what we were made for but have yet to experience.

In the following chapters, we examine Jesus' so-called parable of the prodigal son. We will see Jesus reveal the character of the Father as the family man He alone knows. What we find could not be better news. A loving home and the Father's embrace await. We will also discuss some of the difficulties we have in accepting this good news.

TWO

The Father Jesus Knows

IF WE HAVE no accurate account of the Father, we cannot experience a relationship with Him. I often engage strangers in conversations about God and find that virtually everyone believes in a Supreme Being. Some do not have a clear enough picture of Him to claim a personal relationship, while others legitimately reject the faulty picture they do have. Invariably, the God they turn away from is a cosmic, punitive authority or a non-relational, omnipresent being. Neither group sees the Father Jesus knows. They do not know the Father who loves and likes His children—the well-adjusted parent who is safe to come home to. They have never met the Father revealed by Jesus, the family man who is easy to live with.

The One and Only

The so-called parable of the prodigal son, which we will consider in detail, along with everything else Jesus said and did, should be considered from a dual perspective. He is the smartest person who ever lived; therefore He knows how to get his message across. At the same time, he understands His

Father from the inside and the message He wants us to hear. Think and ponder that for about fifty years, as I have.

"God so loved the world that he gave his one and only Son" (John 3:16). The classical attributes of deity include all-knowing, all-powerful, and all-present. This omnipresent being is everything and everywhere, so what does He lack? The obvious answer is nothing. Think again. He lacks limitation and vulnerability. Complete and changeless from all eternity, He learns nothing and has no place to go.

He had a keen interest in the people He made and watched them as they evolved and progressed. On occasion, He intervened in their history. He could not, however, be a personal participant. He did not experience what it's like to be us, bounded as we are with birth at one end and death at the other.

We face adversity and succeed or fail in confronting it. God does not. We mature and grow, moving from place to place. God does not. We are struck down in mid-life or die of old age. God does not have either experience. That said, we live stories, which are complicated and interesting, in ways God does not.

God watched our stories yet didn't know them from the inside. Then, one member of the Trinitarian family got personally involved. A young Rabbi asked his elder, "Why did God make us?"

The old Rabbi answered, "Because He likes stories." So, God decided to have a human story. His story began here: "The Word became flesh and made his dwelling among us" (John 1:14). The Word who became our flesh lived the most complicated, interesting, and consequential story ever told. In just thirty-three years, Jesus experienced everything we do and much more.

His story became visible at His birth in a goat barn. The one who created earth's atmosphere gasped for His first breath. His teenage peasant mother fed Him from her breasts and changed His diapers. He who spoke the world into being had to learn to talk. He who conversed with the Father and the Spirit had to master people skills.

At about age thirty, Jesus launched His mission into a dangerous environment. In so doing, He experienced the good and bad that we do, and more. Since we have flesh and blood, He, too, shares in our humanity (Hebrews 2:14). He experienced thirst and hunger. He received praise and suffered opposition. He was tempted as we all are (Hebrews 3:18). He knew joy, anger, longing, and disappointment. He had close friends who honored him and close friends who betrayed Him. If you have been betrayed by a loved one, you know it is the worst feeling. Now, God knows how you feel.

Jesus bravely spoke his Father's truth to the religious and political establishment, and they refused to hear Him. Eventually, they killed Him. He was, after all, a limited, vulnerable, and bounded human being with birth at one end and death at the other.

I said earlier that we hear what Jesus said and did from a dual perspective. He is the Word, the Logos, and the ultimate truth of reality who became one of us. He knows us and His Father from the inside; therefore He is uniquely positioned to connect us. The story he told about the father with two sons is beyond mere theological genius. It reveals the heart of true Christianity. We will understand it if we choose to.

When Jesus walked onto the world's stage, announcing, "No one knows the Father except the Son" (Matthew 11:27), and "Anyone who has seen me has seen the Father" (John 14:9), He was essentially saying, "Look no further and look nowhere else. I am who God is. From now on, deduce all you know about Him from Me." Early church theologians understood this critical point and emphasized it in their writings (John 1:18, Colossians 1:15, Hebrews 1:3). Two thousand years later, we, too, must look to Jesus.

In addition to showing us who God the Father is, Jesus

also told stories that reveal additional aspects of His character. The most famous of these is the parable of the prodigal son, found in Luke 15:11–32. It reveals what Jesus means when He says that God is our Father—our Abba, our Daddy. It also reveals what coming home to Him is like.

As you will see, I stay close to the text of Scripture as I discuss what Jesus says about His Father. However, there are other forces at work. The whole issue of a father and a father's relationships to his children is, for me, both rich and problematic. Being a father is the best experience of my life.

I mentioned earlier that last Father's Day all my kids and grandchildren came home to visit me. It was the best day ever. Does the fact that I take delight in my own children affect the way I experience the Father Jesus shows us? Jesus made this comparison: "If you, then, though you are evil, know how to give good gifts to your children, how much more will your Father in heaven give good gifts to those who ask him" (Matthew 7:11). But how much of me do I project onto Him? I suspect that my eagerness to love and give good gifts to my children is only a faint echo of the Father's passion for us. I make this point to emphasize that I am not an objective, dispassionate student of the Father Jesus reveals.

On the other hand, the joy of being a father is the sorrow of having a father who was a disappointment. My parent's marriage broke up when I was young, and my dad divorced me along with my mom. Sixty years has now passed since he left our family, and he has refused to return my calls or answer letters. Does this affect the way I hear Jesus' teaching about my heavenly Father? Being deprived of earthly fatherly love can distort the way we read Scripture. At the same time, it may heighten awareness and intensify discernment that leads to deeper insights.

This chapter introduces themes found in the parable of the two lost sons that reveal the character of our Father and our true home. We will explore these themes in subsequent chapters.

Lost and Found

This story reveals the care of Jesus' mission and the essentials of Christianity. If we are self-aware, we see that it addresses each of us. The father's two sons are different personality types. Generally speaking, we are one or the other at different times during our lives. The prodigal seeks new experiences and is moving toward self-discovery. The elder brother is morally conforming, orderly, and conscientious. Neither is necessarily wrong. Both types of personalities are significant for our growth and understanding of the nature of God.

However, Jesus shows us why both can go wrong. If not properly oriented, the morally conforming, as well as those who pursue self-discovery, can and often do get lost. Jesus precedes his parable of the lost sons by two others: one about a lost sheep and one about a lost coin (Luke 15:3–10). These stories introduce themes that are critical to the central points He makes in the parable of the lost sons. The first theme is that that which is lost is hopelessly lost. What is lost here is a sheep.

I have raised and worked with many farm animals. Sheep are distinguished from other livestock by their helpless vulnerability. If a sheep gets lost in the wilderness, it will die unless rescued. Cows, horses, goats, pigs, and chickens, if lost in the wild, can find their way home or easily adapt to their new, rugged environment. They'll even prosper and multiply. But lose a sheep and that will be the end of that sheep's story.

The next parable of the lost coin makes the same point. A coin that is lost has no power to rescue itself. It is utterly and completely dependent on someone who cares enough to search for it until it is found. Jesus is saying that we are the sheep and the coin. We, too, must be sought for, found, and saved from our blindness and unbelief.

Good News vs. Good Advice

The difference between religion in general and faith in Christ is the difference between good advice and good news. All religion offers some good advice on how to live a better life. Whether it's keeping certain rules about sex, food, taking pilgrimages, meditating, or attempting to be moral, all religions offer at least something of value. But this good advice is all about what we must do to live right and make ourselves acceptable to God and others. Faith in Christ, on the other hand, is not good advice but good news because, as with all news, it is the report of an historical event. In this case, the report of what the Father, through Christ, in the power of the Spirit, has already done to prepare a home for us inside the Trinitarian family. It is good news because it is all about what God does to save us and bring us safely home rather than what we must do to save ourselves.

A few years ago, nine coal miners were trapped underground in a collapsed and flooded mine shaft.[1] They could do nothing to save themselves. Offering advice on how to dig themselves out would have doomed them. They needed rescue, not advice. Their saviors drilled down to where the men were trapped and then lifted each person to safety. This is the rescue mission Jesus highlights in the parables of the lost sheep and the lost coin. It is the good news of how God rescues us and brings us home.

Value in the Eyes of the Beholder

Another central point found in the first two stories sets the stage for the telling of the prodigal story. Both rescuers value that which is lost in ways that make no sense. The shepherd of the first story abandons his ninety-nine sheep "in the open country" (v. 4) and goes looking for the one that is lost. Shepherds are businessmen and unsentimental about their animal inventory. To risk 99 per cent of their net assets by trying to save 1 per cent is nonsense to pragmatic shepherds. We do not see, nor can we guess, why this shepherd acted as he did. All we know is that for whatever reason, the shepherd put a very high value on that one sheep.

In the Gospels, sheep and shepherds are richly textured metaphors rooted in the Old Testament. The first time Jesus appears in John's gospel, He is called "the Lamb of God, who takes away the sin of the world" (John 1:29). Jews reading this knew what it meant. At the time of Moses, after the ten plagues of Egypt, Jews were to splash the blood of a sacrificed lamb on their doors. On the night of the first Passover, the angel of death would see the lamb's blood and pass over that house, sparing those inside. For John's readers, this meant that Jesus, the Lamb, shed His blood to rescue us from spiritual death. To this, John added a second metaphor. In John 10:11, Jesus said, "I am the good shepherd. The good shepherd lays down his life for the sheep." Pulling together these metaphors, we see the Lamb of God and the Good Shepherd meeting in death. Jesus' parable of the shepherd going to all lengths to save one lost sheep now makes more sense in this larger context.

The woman with the irrational attachment to one insignificant coin is like the shepherd risking all to rescue one lost sheep. "Doesn't she light a lamp," spending more on lamp oil than the coin is worth, then "sweep the house and search carefully until she finds it?" (Luke 15:8). Suppose you were standing on a busy street corner, holding something in front of you. As you gaze at the object in your hand, someone bumps you from behind and you drop the object. It disappears into the sewer grate at your feet. You then demand that city officials stop traffic and dig up the grate so you can not only enter the sewer but remain there until your treasure is found. What does this implausible story say about the lost object? It is exceedingly valuable, as you are to God. He sees us as treasures of immense and irreplaceable worth. God is expert at finding the lost and bringing them home. In fact, His Son defined His mission in these words: "For the Son of Man came to seek and save the lost" (Luke 19:10).

The irrational and impractical shepherd and the compulsive woman point to the father in Jesus' final story. He, representing our Father in heaven, values that which is lost to him. As we shall see, the father's two sons are a pair of the worst characters Jesus could have described. Each gets lost in his own way. The father successfully rescues one son. The story ends with his attempt to save the second. All three stories—the lost sheep, the lost coin, and the two lost sons—show that the Father loves us without cause and for no reason other than it is the way He is. The counterpoint, which is covered later in this book, is that He fully intends for us to trust Him and love Him back. A true relationship with God is one of reciprocity.

A Mixed Crowd

A mixed crowd gathers around Jesus to hear this first telling of the parable of the prodigal son. Religious rule keepers and irreligious rule breakers rub shoulders as Jesus weaves a tale that includes and exposes both groups. The "Pharisees and teachers of the law" (Luke 15:2) stand proud as the religious rule keepers and moral conformists, like the elder brother in the story. "Tax collectors and sinners (Luke 15:1)," are well known as the rule breakers and are easily identified as the prodigal himself.

Jesus tells the parable in response to the complaints of the religious rule keepers. What is their accusation? "This man welcomes sinners and eats with them" (Luke 15:2). We can fully appreciate their complaint only by knowing the significance of table fellowship in the ancient Near East. Even today, in some cultures, sharing a meal with others is a way to honor and identify with them. The text states specifically that Jesus welcomed and received sinners as well as ate with them. This means that it was Jesus Himself who hosted these fellowship meals. He was the one who invited the guests and served the wine and food. It is He who welcomed them home to Himself, His Heavenly Father, and the fellowship of the Spirit.

A rabbi who shared food from a common dish with notorious sinners would have been highly offensive to the religious moralists because they thought evil could be transported through food and drink and would, therefore, spread contamination. They practiced social distancing as we did during the Covid-19 pandemic. If Jesus merely taught people about tolerating sinners, there would have been little concern. The real problem arose because He actually welcomed them, received them, and dined with them. The religious leaders branded sinners—like tax collectors and harlots—as enemies of God and demanded strict separation from them. Many of us have heard and believed the same lie that a holy God must distance Himself from sinners, especially the unrepentant.

When Jesus declared solidarity with outcasts by eating with them, He said they were totally accepted by Him and His Father. They were already included prior to repentance or any act of restitution, which the teachers required. Therefore, since the religious leaders rejected sinners, they also rejected Jesus, who was in solidarity with them. He left the Pharisees no choice but to change everything they believed or to reject Him. They chose to reject Jesus.

Tension brewed as Jesus told his edgy story. He stated that the father doesn't have just one son—the good one—but two —a rule keeper and a rule breaker. The story ends with a feast of celebration (15:32) to which both sons are welcomed and encouraged to join. Jesus' punch line cuts to the quick by proclaiming that both sons are equally bad, equally lost, yet equally valued, loved, and accepted. With one stroke, Jesus destroyed the Pharisees' entire worldview, which is based on the notion that God divides the world into two groups: the good and the bad. I discuss this dualism in chapter 6. The story turned this worldview upside down, placing the self-proclaimed insider elder brothers outside and looking in. The parable ends in suspense: Will the moral, rule-keeping outsider come in and join the celebration? Or will he remain on the outside?

The Prodigal's Demand

"Give me my share of the estate," the younger son demands of his father. "So he divided his property between them" (Luke 15:12). We will consider the cruel insult of the prodigal's request later. For now, let us reflect upon the father's response.

In our church, we sing a song that contains the line "God is in control." This is a comforting notion, but one that needs qualifying. Fathers in Jesus' day were absolute monarchs. They had total control over their families and finances. The father in Jesus' parable exercises his sovereign control by relinquishing it. Control in its usual sense implies the effective use of force to produce a desired result. By force, we hammer nails, incarcerate criminals, and win wars. Force is good for doing physical work. But there is a kind of work that we cannot do by force. It is the work of maintaining relationships between free persons.

Think of it this way: If we want someone to do or not do something, we may try persuasion. If that fails, we can attempt manipulation. If that doesn't work, and if we have the means, we can apply coercion. The father had all these options, and he chose his son's freedom instead.

When the father tells his son to, "Take the money. Go, if you wish," we see that freedom for his son is more desirable to him than maintaining control over family and financial affairs.

He, no doubt, does not want to lose half his estate. Nor does he welcome the cruel insult and public humiliation that result from his son's actions. We assume that sorrow engulfs him as he watches his son wander into the pagan degradation of the far country and becomes lost. Like our Father in heaven, he has the power, authority, and right to control but chooses his child's freedom instead. He allows his son the liberty to stay or go, to love or reject. The rest of the parable explains why a relationship of reciprocal love with his children is the father's goal. Freedom is the means. The father values freedom, not as a good in itself, but rather to make possible the good he seeks. C. S. Lewis wrote, "Why did God give them free will? Because free will, though it makes evil possible, is also the only thing that makes possible any love or goodness or joy worth having."[2] Freedom means the relationship is based on love and not on force, fear, coercion, or cultish religion.

Some would argue that to suggest God does not control all events undermines His glory. I disagree. In my opinion, there is nothing glorious about sheer power. Praiseworthy glory has to do with character. Parents or religious leaders who exercise meticulous control over their children or followers, hoping to ensure that things go exactly as they want, are insecure, weak, and ineffective. On the other hand, leaders who influence others by the force of their own loving character gain respect and admiration. The Father Jesus knows has all power. For the sake of winning our love, He limits His "all power," allowing us the freedom to choose between good and evil, love and the rejection of love. Those who live at peace in the Father's home are there voluntarily.

As the story unfolds, it is apparent that the father wants the son's love. But love is only possible when it is given. In order to get a voluntary *yes*, the father must first risk an insulting *no*. Some have suggested that it is a strange kind of love that enables a foolish child to make bad choices that result in suffering. However, the freedom to choose the objects of our affection is foundational to love itself. The son chooses to reject his father while the father maintains his child as the object of his affection. This choice is made out of freedom and sovereign love. It depends upon nothing.

Freedom to Suffer

The prodigal now liquidates his share of the estate and runs to the far country. He wastes the money and spends his energy on reckless living. We will discuss the consequences of this misuse of freedom later, but for now note that the father does not run after the prodigal. Rather, he models respect for the son and cooperates with an underlying truth inherent in freedom. He stays put and allows the foolish young man to experience the consequences of freedom.

As a father, I know how difficult this can be. My natural inclination is to guide my children's choices rather than give them the dignity of becoming agents in their own learning. Watching them be hurt by making poor decisions is agony. But if I interfere or interfere too often, I will sacrifice something essential and beautiful: their own personhood and their freedom to explore and discover who they are and what the world is like. The world is dangerous, and they should learn that at an early age. They also need to learn that making good choices offers some protection.

One important lesson the prodigal learns is that freedom to sin is not freedom at all. Nowhere in the New Testament is sin equated with freedom. It is always seen as bondage or, as I say elsewhere, it violates the structures of reality. The prodigal learns this the hard way. Upon his return, he also learns that submitting to what the father wants for him is the only true freedom available. The freedom to choose guarantees one will face consequences. Consequences are sometimes painful, and surviving them may seem unlikely, but the father in this story no doubt hopes his boy will learn from his mistakes and discover who he is and what the real world is like.

The Complete Parent

This father is not your typical dad. He exceeds cultural norms. He is endowed with the best of traditional fatherly traits, and the best motherly traits as well. Here, I reflect upon His maternal traits as revealed by Jesus. (It may be of interest to note that the Hebrew word for the Spirit of God in the Old Testament is most often feminine.)

We commonly refer to a mother as being the "heart of the home." Her sympathetic glance and supportive touch stand in contrast to a father's sometimes stern demands. When sons go bad, they often face their father's wrath, but a mother has a way of sticking by her children no matter what. Those of us who visit prisoners in jail see mostly mothers in the visiting room. They leave their coats and hats and dreams of what their sons might have become, while the guard watches at the gate. The most famous mother of all stuck by her convict son and laid her dreams at the foot of a Roman cross. Mothers often remain long after friends and partners depart.

The father in Jesus' story illustrates the best of a mother's unconditional loyalty as he watches and waits for his prodigal to return. Sighting his son in the distance, he runs to meet him, showers him with kisses and hugs, dresses him properly, and feeds him a hot meal. These are all acts of kindness associated with good mothers. His maternal heart comes into stark focus in Luke 15:20. He sees the boy off in the distance and has "compassion" on him. This New Testament word opens a window into the depths of God's emotional life. It refers to bowels or viscera. It denotes emotional violence. Our term "gut-wrenching" is close to the New Testament understanding of this word. It is the involuntary gasp of someone overwhelmed by a great sorrow or the groan of a woman in labor.

The Hebrew background of this word is *womb*, referring to the vivid, intense flood of tenderness an expectant mother feels for the child in her belly. It is an emotion most closely associated with the feminine. This combination of anguish and tenderness is what seizes the father at the sight of his returning son. It is here, as in many other places, that Scripture corrects the traditional theological assertion that God is aloof from what we call feelings.[3]

The revelation that deep compassion is what moves God to action is not new information in Jesus' parable. The prophets before him painted vivid pictures of the profound emotional life of God. One such portrayal is found in Isaiah 49. Beginning in verse 8, the Lord sings affirmations and lavish promises of restoration over Israel, reaching a kind of crescendo in verse 13: "Shout for joy, you heavens; rejoice, you earth; burst into song, you mountains! For the LORD comforts his people and will have compassion on his afflicted ones." (Note: The Old Testament word for compassion is the same for womb.)

But right at this point, Israel interrupts and states, "The LORD has forsaken me, the Lord has forgotten me" (v. 14). Like a petulant child refusing a parent's comfort, Israel insists that she is forsaken and forgotten.

The Lord then patiently explains why it is impossible for Him to forget or forsake His children:

"Can a mother forget the baby at her breast and have no compassion on the child she has born?" (v. 15).

What was it in the relationship between a nursing mother and her baby that should have consoled Israel in their fear that the Lord had forsaken them?

I happen to know a lot about nursing mothers and their devotion to the babes at their breasts. I've led six churches over the past fifty years that were filled with nursing mothers. I am also married to Patti, who nursed our eight children for a total of eighteen years. Here is some of what I've learned.

A mother's tenderness and love for her nursing baby is

chemically hardwired. When the baby sucks and letdown of the mother's milk occurs, a rush of hormones flood the mother's brain and produce profound feelings of affection. This process works in reverse also. For some women, a tender glance at an infant is all it takes to trigger these hormones that get the milk flowing. The Lord, of course, possesses no body and is not subject to the rush of mood-altering chemicals. However, the picture He paints of Himself in Isaiah 49 shows the compassion He feels for us (vv. 10, 13, 15).

Western theological tradition leaves little room for the emotional life of God. I have discussed this at length in my book *Authority to Heal.*[4] Here, let me simply say that our lack of appreciation for God's emotions is due to traditional theism taking the attributes of God and recasting them in abstract Greek philosophical terms. For instance, God's impassibility came to mean that God cannot be emotionally moved by us. Augustine said that God does not grieve over our suffering. St. Anselm of Canterbury followed suit, stating that God experiences no compassion for us. As God's emotional life was minimized, we also lost His relationality. As Walter Kasper puts it, classical theism presents God as a "solitary narcissistic being who suffers from his own completeness."[5] Dallas Willard added, "I was raised in a theology that presents God as a great unblinking cosmic stare."[6] But the Father / Mother Jesus knows corrects these errors and opens our hearts to Him and summons us.

The God reflected in Isaiah 49 is clearly relational. A nursing mother must meet the needs of her child. While the baby obviously needs the nourishment, the mother needs the child to drink regularly or she will suffer the pain of engorged breasts. Patti often reached for her babies not because they were crying or needed to be fed, but because she wanted relief from the pressure of the bounty filling her breasts. Theologians who oppose the notion that God has a true emotional life tend also to object to the idea that God might be moved to act toward us out of any need or must of His own. This is certainly true of the "unblinking cosmic stare" of Western theology. But the God Jesus reveals is the relationally rich family of Father, Son, and Spirit. This God is the Good Shepherd, the nursing Mother, the waiting Father. The Father Jesus knows not only loves us but feels love for us.

Theological abstractions about deity are easily qualified by the teaching of Jesus. In our parable the father says, "we had to celebrate and be glad" (Luke 15:32)" because his son came home. Here, the Father acts in accordance with an imperative of His own desire and a need to extend mercy. How quickly this view of God transforms our mindset regarding spiritual disciplines. Reading the Bible and prayer are no longer arduous, one-sided religious duties; instead, they are channels of nourishment for us and opportunities of relief for God to let down His bounty. They are means of releasing the abundant life of home.

Keeping a baby fed is a time-consuming, energy-sapping operation. A woman who nurses her child has chosen a relationship of unconditional commitment that is rarely seen in any other human relationship. Every friendship is to some degree reciprocal. Each party contributes at least something to the mix. If not, the friendship dissolves. Every marriage is reciprocal to a degree. If one spouse gives everything and the other gives nothing, though they are still formally married, in reality the union ceases. Every human relationship hangs in this balance of give and take—except that of the nursing mother and her child. She gives it all: the substance of her body, the vigilant attention of her thoughts, and the possibility of a peaceful night of sleep. And what does baby give back? The baby can only continue to need, demand, and take.

The God Isaiah proclaimed gave it all as well. His children had been faithless and disloyal. They grieved Him continually. Their worship was shallow and calculating. They gave nothing He desired; yet He loved them. Why? Because God is like a mother with a babe at the breast. The father Jesus described gives it all too. In true motherly fashion, He does all he can to get his children home with him.

While fathers aren't hardwired to their children in the same way mothers are, many of us fathers have at least tasted that gut-wrenching compassion the father had for his prodigal son.

When our first daughter, Haven, was two years old, I lost her on a crowded San Diego beach. We had five kids then, and to my credit, I knew where the other four were, but the blond-haired girl in the little red bathing suit was gone. I tried to remain composed, thinking she must be close by, hiding behind an umbrella or curled up under a towel. But a minute's scan of both sand and sea dissolved my efforts in a flood of fear. Shrieking her name, demanding assistance, and suspecting everyone of taking her, I attracted a crowd but not my little girl.

Question: How long does it take a father to lose his mind and choke on his heart?

Answer: As long as it takes to lose a curious toddler.

My story has a happy ending. A blond-haired girl in a little red bathing suit was soon spotted across the street, and Haven was quickly rescued from a playground full of happy children. Reunited with her brothers, she ran off on her next adventure, while I struggled to gain control of my bowels. The ghost pains of that day still haunt my gut and cause me to wonder about our heavenly Father whose children continually lose themselves.

Lost and Don't Know It?

Being lost and knowing it is a terrifying experience. Being lost and not knowing it is more serious. My wife stood fishing on the bank of the river while our new baby slept snuggly against her in the tummy pack. Norm, our friend and guide, kept an eye on her from upstream as I set off confidently toward the car to retrieve the forgotten lunch. Norm's tales of lost hikers roaming the dense Manitoba woods and never finding their way out didn't concern me. I knew my way around, and twenty minutes later I was at the car tucking food into my pack. I proudly reentered the woods and imagined the river dead ahead. Because of my recent navigational success, I allowed myself the luxury of taking a look around. The solitude and beauty of the wilderness inspired peaceful contemplation as I happily dodged trees and jumped logs—until I realized that the twenty-minute walk out had become a ninety-minute trek back into the very same woods Norm's poor hikers roamed. How is it that being lost, and becoming increasingly more so, could have been so nonchalantly enjoyed? Simple. I didn't know I was lost and had no clue that I needed to be found. Fortunately, Norm eventually found me; otherwise, I would not have been able to write this book and tell you how easy it is to get lost.

Those who know they are lost and those who don't have a clue mingle around Jesus as He tells His story. This includes the sinners and tax collectors, the prodigals who are already finding their way home, the Pharisees, and the elder brothers who are lost and don't know it.

Getting Found

The parable of the prodigal son ends well; he gets found. Jesus tells of his homecoming in Luke 15:20–24. We aren't told how long the son was in the far country. We don't know how long it took to "come to his senses" (v. 17). He must have known the ruckus his departure caused. Offending the patriarch and hightailing it out of town would have been an affront to the whole community. Scholars suggest that in order for the prodigal to reach his father's home, he might first have to walk through town. Aware of the highly offended people along the route, who were more than likely intent on defending the honor of the rejected patriarch, the sharp-eyed father ran to intercept his returning prodigal. There on the outskirts of town, compassion is translated into a series of actions that demonstrate just how loved and welcomed the boy is.

We witness the first public display of the father's excesses as he raises his robes and begins to run. Jesus' listeners would understand this to mean that the father is excited, but they would be shocked by his behavior. A patriarch doesn't run— for any reason. Children run, and slaves hurry from task to task, but a nobleman's status dictates that he only walks while in the public eye. The sight of an elderly nobleman, legs flying beneath his upraised robe, would be embarrassing and obscene. But this father is willing to sacrifice every shred of personal dignity to reach his child quickly. Many of us think of God as a judge who is quick to find fault, to shame, and to punish. Jesus says not so. He is quick to run, embrace, and welcome home.

Imagine the father winded and breathing hard as he falls on his son's neck and kisses him. The Greek word used here, *katephilēsen*, actually means "to kiss repeatedly." This passionate embrace and shower of kisses is more than an over-flow of relief and affection. It both protects the son from any physical hostility that might come from the community and prevents him from falling on his knees to, at least symbolically, humble himself by kissing his father's hands or feet. Though expected of children and junior family members in such situa-tions, this father does not allow the subservient bow.

At first, the prodigal can't see the message in his father's behavior. He brushes the expressive outpouring of affection aside and tries to deliver what sounds like a canned speech. As we shall see later, this speech is not repentance. It is merely a request for a job. He says what he thinks he should say to get some food. I make this point to show that everything the father gives his son is not in response to the prodigal meeting any conditions. The boy does nothing to prompt the father's blessing. Everything is given gratuitously. All for nothing. The father's love, like that of a nursing mother, is unconditional and unmerited. "Father, I have sinned," the boy states (v. 21). But the father isn't listening. I like to picture him putting his hand over the boy's mouth or shutting him up by covering his lips with more kisses.

It was enough just to come home. The prodigal gets found and the father does the rest. "Bring the best robe and put it on him," he commands (v. 22). The best robe is the father's own garment. From now on, wherever the son goes, he will be clothed in the father's protection and honor. "Put a ring on his finger and sandals on his feet" (v. 21), laughs the happy and exuberant daddy as he reestablishes his son as a member of the family—all rights intact. It is likewise enough that we just come home. The Father Jesus takes care of the rest. "Having predestined us to be His own adopted children by Jesus Christ, according to the good pleasure of His will, to the praise of the glory of His grace, wherein He hath made us accepted in His Beloved: in Whom we have redemption through His blood, the forgiveness of sins, according to the richness of His grace" (Ephesians 1:5–7 TMB).

And now it's time to feast. "Bring the fattened calf," he commands. "It is time to celebrate (Luke 15:23)." A sheep or goat would be appropriate for a family dinner, but a fattened calf would require at least one hundred people to consume it. He orders a feast for the entire town and intends to reconcile his son to the whole community. Such feasts were exceptional. They were reserved to honor kings or high-ranking govern-mental officials or as part of the eldest son's wedding. By throwing such an extravagant party, the father honors his son in a most dramatic way.

The common name of this parable is the parable of the

prodigal son. This misleads. Jesus begins his story in Luke 15:11 by saying, "There was a man who had two sons." There are three main characters, and there is more than one prodigal. The most significant prodigal is the father. The word prodigal does not mean wayward. The dictionary defines *prodigal* as "reckless spendthrift, foolishly extravagant, spending everything." The term is appropriate to the father who spends lavishly for the younger son's initial freedom and again when he returns. Jesus shows God's reckless grace, which is our greatest hope. There was a dark Friday afternoon, two thousand years ago when the Father spent it all. For three days, heaven was bankrupt.

Always a Son

Continuing our earlier discussion of freedom, we see now that if we, like the prodigal, use our freedom to reject God, He does not, in turn, reject us. Our parable is about a son who remains a son because his father remains his father and his home remains his home. The robe, the ring, the sandals, and the celebration not only reflect the grace of the father but also reiterate the truth of who the son is. He discovers that he was always the son, despite his sin, simply because his father never ceased being his father. True, the prodigal squanders his material inheritance and will not get another. It's a fact; there are serious and sometimes lifelong consequences for bad choices and violating the structures of reality. However, there remains an inheritance he cannot lose: he has a father and a home forever. There is only so much damage we can do to ourselves.

To paint a picture updated for modern eyes, a man left home when he was sixteen and hadn't communicated with his parents since. The life he led resulted in arrest and imprisonment for over a decade. When he was released from prison, he was out of options, except to write his parents and ask if he could come home. He said he would understand if they didn't want to see him. He explained that on a certain date he would ride a city bus that passed their house. If they were willing to see him, they could tie a yellow ribbon to a branch of the oak tree in the front yard. If he saw the yellow ribbon, he would get off the bus. If there was no ribbon, he would keep going. On the appointed day, he rode the bus, feeling afraid to look. But when he did, there wasn't one yellow ribbon. Instead, the tree was covered with over a hundred yellow ribbons. It's like that.

The Father's Two Sons

We know that the young prodigal accepts his sonship because the party happens. "He was lost and is found. So they began to celebrate" (v. 24). This sounds like a good place to end the story. Jesus has provided some controversial assertions about God. True, some of what He says is offensive, but it is all worth mulling over. But then, as though turning a page and exposing the punch line, Jesus takes His time and subtly reminds us that the father in the parable has two sons. "Meanwhile, the older son was in the field. . . . [He] became angry and refused to go in. So his father went out and pleaded with him" (vv. 25, 28).

Earlier that day, the father ran for his young prodigal. Now he goes out to find the elder. By going after both of them, Jesus tears the curtain of moral judgment that separates Pharisees from sinners. Careful listeners are drawn to the conclusion that although the elder son works hard at doing what he thinks is right, he has, just like his little brother, distanced himself from his father. We will discuss at length how we can separate ourselves from God through rule keeping as well as rule breaking later. But for now, the point is that ultimately it matters little whether we separate from God through immorality or morality.

The path the elder son walks to the celebration is a step-by-step parallel of the younger son's long journey home. First, he approaches the house from the fields, where he has been working as a servant, just as his brother had returned from the far country, working as a servant. Next, the father runs out to meet him, just as he had the prodigal. And finally, the father is dishonored again, not by greed this time, but by a son's self-righteous defiance.

Both sons rebel against the father and get lost. One runs from home and gets totally lost in the far country. The other stays home and manages to get spiritually and relationally lost. For the second time in one day, the father goes out to "seek and to save the lost" (Luke 19:10).

We have considered the character of the Father and what it is like coming home to Him. Let us now take a closer look at his two sons and as we do, also take a closer look at ourselves.

THREE

The Prodigal

THIS CHAPTER FOLLOWS the prodigal's journey from home, into the far country, and back again. The next chapter looks at the elder brother. With little imagination, we may be able to identify with each son. I certainly do.

The overview of the prodigal's story goes like this: The young man wants his freedom. He wants to pursue the pleasures of life on his terms away from his true home, so he demands his share of the estate to finance his endeavor. His father grants his son the independence he desires and loads him down with resources. His son tries to make a home for himself in an alien environment and learns that the far country is not the right place for him. He doesn't belong. It goes against his grain. It's not home.

The father gives freedom and resources; the son misuses them and suffers as a result. But none of it is wasted. In the process of behaving badly and experiencing consequences, the prodigal gains valuable lessons about the cause-and-effect universe in which he lives. Aiming at self-discovery without a proper orientation proved disastrous.

I know from personal experience the results of poor impulse control. In my youth, I sought short-term pleasure without considering long-term consequences. In my late teens, I consumed drugs and was sexually active simply because it felt good. I wrecked my life, and someone died as a result. My pagan lifestyle got me lost in a prodigal sort of way. Then the Good Shepherd found me and bore me home. The details of this chapter of my life are found in my book, *The Divine Project: Live Your Best Story.*

I used to go deep-sea fishing off the coast of British Columbia with my friend Dave. He was a single, free-spirited young man who lived on his boat and fished for salmon and halibut just often enough to pay the bills and buy food. When I asked why he chose this life, he boasted, "Out on the ocean I am free from all rules. There are no traffic lights out here. I can go in any direction I want as far as I want. No one tells me what I can and cannot do."

Well, I became envious of that kind of freedom. As the pastor of a growing church, I worked over sixty hours a week. Some of my time was spent studying, writing sermons, and praying, but most of it was filled with scheduled and unscheduled meetings. Everyone had an opinion about what I could and couldn't do. How refreshing it would be to be free from all the rules. The more time I spent with Dave, though, the more I realized his so-called freedom was an illusion. He was fixated on tidal charts. He listened constantly to ever-changing weather reports on his shortwave radio. He was dedicated to coastal maps. There may not have been traffic lights, but Dave knew he sailed on an unforgiving sea with inherent rules of its own.

It is not difficult to imagine the prodigal, his back to the door, defiantly declaring there are no rules out there—no one to tell him what he can and can't do. "I will go in any direction as far as I want," he likely stated. But he soon discovers the inherent rules of the universe in which he lives, or, as I often say, the structures of reality. He learns that the rules of reality must be obeyed or destruction and poverty is the result. In the far country, he discovers that the gift of freedom is real and also dangerous.

After he misuses and loses his wealth, the inherent rules of the universe take hold. "There was a severe famine in that whole country, and he began to be in need" (Luke 15:14). Life for the young adventurer goes from bad to worse; eventually, he joins himself to a citizen of the alien country who sends him out to feed the pigs (v. 15). The word to *join* means "to cling to, to closely associate with or to make a home with." When the prodigal, who is a Jew, joins himself to and makes his home with a pagan employer, he has turned as far from his father's home as possible. Jewish abhorrence of pigs is well known. It is recorded in the famous Talmud: "Cursed is the man who breeds swine."[1] Kenneth Baily explains the breaking this oath this more clearly: "The result of his lostness was that he exchanged living in his father's palace for living in the wilderness, and the companionship of his family for the companionship of pigs."[2]

It would seem that the son's downward movement has run its course. His degradation, however, goes even deeper before he comes to his senses and heads for home. Jesus says the boy longed to eat what the pigs ate. Remember the significance table fellowship has already played in this story? The religious leaders are upset with Jesus because he eats with and therefore declares solidarity with tax collectors and sinners. In this culture, table companions define you. Who defines the prodigal in this alien family? He longs to share the food of pigs. A once-noble Jewish boy arrives at a place where little separates him from unclean animals. His desire for freedom and his attempt to make a home for himself apart from his father ends as badly as can be imagined. "Do not be deceived: God cannot be mocked. A man reaps what he sows" (Galatians 6:7). We live in a consequential universe!

The prodigal finally learns what he needs to about disoriented self-discovery and the far country. He comes to his senses and returns home. He is met with forgiveness, love, and total acceptance despite his betrayal. The essence of grace is that we are repeatedly let off the hook. We are not punished for our sins, but because we live in a consequential world, we are always punished *by* the sins. The son learns there is grace in his father's home and only consequences at the pig farm.

Another aspect of the prodigal's story reveals how the love, joy, and pleasure we seek can only be found in the environment the Father gives. The prodigal asks for his share of the father's estate so he can spend it on "wild living" (v. 13). When I was younger, that sounded exciting. Now, I know better. The young man was bent on finding pleasure on his own terms. I have lived long enough to recognize this as a recipe for disaster.

Pursuing happiness and pleasure is not wrong in itself. We are created by God to do just that. As Karl Barth observed, "The will to life is the will for joy and happiness. . . . It is hypocrisy to hide this from oneself."[3] We exit the womb with our core longings switched on. The need for acceptance and love are driving inner forces from the start. When these desires are met, we feel pleasure. When they are not, we are frustrated.

God created us to long for happiness. And being good, He plans to satisfy these longings. Further, He plans that our deepest longings for pleasure be satisfied at home with Him. The psalmist experienced this reality. Addressing our Father, he says: "You make known to me the path of life. You will fill me with joy in your presence, with eternal pleasures at your right hand" (Psalm 16:11).

We should not fault the prodigal for seeking self-discovery or pleasure. We should, however, view him as foolish for seeking it in the wrong place. Away from home in the far country, he is out of his element like a fish out of water. He doesn't fit there and cannot thrive. He goes against his own grain in the pursuit of pleasure, and it ends badly.

Throughout the Bible, in hundreds of ways, God assures

us that our longings for life and joy are good and that He provides a place for those longings to be satisfied. The wise man who penned Proverbs 5:18–20, for instance, celebrates the pleasure of sex as he warns that sex can be safely enjoyed only at home where it is designed to work.

> "May your fountain be blessed, and may you rejoice in the wife of your youth. . . . May her breasts satisfy you always, may you ever be intoxicated with her love. Why my son, be intoxicated with another man's wife? Why embrace the bosom of a wayward woman?"

Just so, the prodigal sought pleasure away from his father's home, and for a time he seemed to find it. A fish out of water, however, does not live long. "He sought pleasure, he found pain. He wished for freedom and got bondage." [4]

In simple language, sin is pleasure that is bad for us, while virtue is pleasure that is good for us. If that doesn't sound right, then you probably have not yet had enough experience with either. Experience finally teaches this dual wisdom.

For the prodigal and for us, it is good that sin hurts and that turning from the Father and home is punishing. It is to our advantage that rebellion leaves us feeling used up and empty. The broken promises of freedom and pleasure in the far country turn many of us back to where we belong. At home, the prodigal receives for free everything he vainly sought to acquire where he didn't fit. Back in his element and like a fish returned to the water, he is positioned to thrive. No longer going against his own grain, he is set to flourish; in time, he will learn what true freedom and the deepest pleasures in life truly are.

Repentance: The Way Home?

It is traditionally taught that the story turns when the prodigal "came to his senses" (Luke 15:17). He then asks, "How many of my father's hired servants have food to spare, and here I am starving to death! I will set out and go back to my father and say to him: Father I have sinned against heaven and against you. I am no longer worthy to be called your son; make me like one of your hired servants. So he got up and went to his father" (vv. 17–20). The conventional teaching is that here the sinner repents, sees the error of his ways, feels sorry about what he has done, and is ready to make amends, thus accomplishing the work that must be done in order to change the father's attitude toward him and bring about reconciliation.

The unknown author of the Christian classic *The Whole Duty of Man* summarized the traditional view of repentance. "There is no promise of forgiveness of any sin but only to him who confesseth it and forsaketh it." Anything short of this kind of repentance "will never avail him toward his pardon."[5] Following this line of thought, a friend of mine recently preached a sermon on the prodigal son, titled, "If You Repent, Then God Will Forgive." In the body of the sermon, he stated, "Before you repent, God is your Judge. After you repent, He is your Savior."

I have most often heard the parable and repentance handled this way in general. Pastoral and theological problems that flow from this are significant. First, how does anyone ever know if they have repented properly or enough? Must we be sincere? How do we know we are sincere enough? If we have to do something and do it correctly for God to accept us, how can we ever know it worked? There will be no assurance. Secondly, the idea that God's attitude toward us needs to change and that we hold the key to that change is a problem. It implies there is something we can do to alter the being and character of God from Judge to Savior. It suggests that God is waiting for us to do something to change His mind and attitude toward us.

Another problem is that while the parable of the prodigal is about repentance, nothing like the traditional view is revealed in the story. The text itself takes us in a different direction. Stand back and look again at the three parables that represent being lost: the sheep, the coin, and the sons. It is clear the common religious understanding of repentance is nowhere to be found. In fact, Jesus highlights repentance as something radically unlike the traditional view.

THE LOST SHEEP: Jesus affirms that the point of this parable is repentance. "There will be more rejoicing in heaven over one sinner who repents than over ninety-nine righteous persons who do not need to repent" (Luke 15:7). The lost and found sheep is clearly a symbol of repentance. But how so? A sheep gets lost, a shepherd goes the distance to find it, and there is rejoicing at the outcome. What exactly is Jesus' radical view of repentance? The answer: something that is lost gets found.

THE LOST COIN: It's the same story. A coin gets lost, a woman finds it, then she calls for a celebration. Jesus reiterates, "There is rejoicing in the presence of the angels of God over one sinner who repents" (Luke 15:10). There is no way a sheep or a coin can be credited with the awareness of sin or heartfelt confession of traditional, religious repentance, yet they both represent repentance. Why? Something lost gets found.

The prodigal does not repent in the traditional sense. There is no lowered head or trembling voice confessing a big mistake or sorrow regarding his actions. He isn't ashamed of the pain he

causes or the financial loss. He moseys off like the sheep and
strolls back, still lost and looking for food. And then he gets
found. Once again, Jesus teaches, through the father of the
prodigal son, that repentance is the key: "We had to celebrate
and be glad, because this brother of yours was dead and is alive
again; he was lost and is found" (Luke 15:31–32). He also
gave the command to "kill the fattened calf for him!" (v. 30).
He hadn't changed from bad to now good—from defiant to
now sorry. He was simply lost and is now found. To his credit,
like the sheep hung up in the bush or stuck in a rut, the
prodigal at the edge of town participates by allowing himself
to get found.

It's the same message three times over. Kenneth Bailey was
the Middle Eastern missionary scholar who wrote more about
this parable than anyone else. He said that to teach the religious view of repentance from the son's decision to come
home is "perhaps the most theologically damaging traditional
misunderstanding of this parable. . . . When understood in
this fashion, the text loses its cutting edge, and the theological
unity of the chapter is broken."[6]

The cutting edge and theological unity of this chapter is
the revelation of what true repentance is and how it happens.
The God figures—the shepherd, the woman, and the father—
take the initiative. They do all the seeking and saving. That
which is lost is found and brought home.

The father's attitude and character are stable and consistent. Nothing the son does changes him. Letting himself be
found means that it is he who changes. Repentance is happen-
ing. For us, this means there is nothing we can do or not do to
alter our Father's attitude toward us. Repentance at our end
does not mean that we have made things right with God; it
means we believe in his unflinching love for us and have
accepted it on his terms. That is to say, we accept our
acceptance.

Commenting on repentance, C. S. Lewis wrote, "It is not

something God demands of you before he will take you back . . . it is simply a description of what going back is like."[7] Once back, there is often conviction of sin, a real sense of guilt, confession, and moral reform. This more traditional view of repentant behavior is not the cause but the fruit of a stable, established relationship with the Father Jesus knows.

Repentance in the New Testament means to change your mind and agenda. Repentance toward God means to change the way we think about God and the way we relate to Him.

Jesus proclaimed in Mark 1:15, "The kingdom of God has come near. Repent and believe the good news!" In other words, you believe bad news about God and his kingdom, so change your mind about Him and change the ways you are trying to relate to Him. He is not saying forsake your private sins and close the moral gap between you and the Holy God. He says the kingdom is near. Accept your place in God's family now. As Kenneth Bailey put it: "For first-century Judaism, repentance was a way of bringing in the kingdom. In the preaching of Jesus, repentance was a response to the kingdom already come through him."[8] Religious repentance does not close a gap between God and us because there is no gap.

Jesus now brings the most significant aspect of the prodigal's story into focus. When the son comes home, he discovers that, in a sense, it's as if he never left. The gap he thought existed between him and his father was never real.

Imagine the father on his porch, watching the road, recalling the day his son left. One hand shades his eyes. He sees movement on the horizon. Someone is walking down the hill into town. Could it be him, finally? No. Too skinny and no swagger. But as the walking man gets closer and turns to look over his shoulder, the father sees the distinct profile of his boy. The father runs. He crashes into his son, almost knocking him over, breathing hard, embracing him. This is repentance. Someone lost is found.

Kindness Leads to Repentance

The prodigal receives the father's embrace, the robe, the ring, and the sandals. This is symbolic of repentance having happened. According to Paul, "God's kindness is intended to lead you to repentance" (Romans 2:4).

Since saviors do all the work and pay all the cost, does this mean we are completely passive in the drama of reconciliation? Not at all. As we receive our Father's embrace, we embrace Him back. In reflecting on the return of the prodigal, Miroslav Volf shows us what it's like.[9] "The drama of reconciliation begins as the father runs with open arms to his child. Before the son can say or do anything, the father makes clear his intentions. Open arms say I want you close. I don't want to wait. There are no conditions to meet first." The father sees his son in the distance and starts running. He doesn't know why the prodigal returns. Maybe the boy has not changed, or maybe he has changed for the worse. It doesn't matter because he is found. But the father's love is not enough. His longing to be close and to reconcile will be satisfied only when his son returns the embrace. We have all hugged people who didn't hug back. When this happens, we know that we have not really connected. The return of an embrace is like the closing of the circuit that turns on the light. The father's open arms and open heart declare that there are no gaps between him and his boy. He is saying clearly that it's safe to come home. The whole town can see the father giving it his all, but this powerful embrace will never reach its goal until the son embraces him back.

This, now, is the critical point in the life of the prodigal. The father cannot grasp the son against his will. If the prodigal returns his father's embrace, then true repentance has occurred, and the story will end happily for both. If he does not, then the father's gamble on grace will have exposed his intent, but not won his son. The prodigal's presence at the celebration that soon follows reveals that the father did, in fact, win his boy. His grace triumphed! It's the power of a mutual embrace and bond. The son returns to his true home. The prodigal finds his home the way he left it. Everything looks the same and feels the same. The only thing that changed is his heart. The father has repented him. Now he is different.

The Prodigal Is Transformed

Two things we all want are acceptance and change. We want to be accepted just as we are, but we don't want to stay the way we are. We want to be better. This story shows that the father gives both. The son is accepted; he hugs back and then begins to change. The secret to his transformation is the same as his acceptance. The father simply will not let go of his child.

The prodigal set off to the far country to make a home among aliens. He comes crawling back, asking only for a job and food. As his father approaches, the prodigal begins his prepared speech but is interrupted with an emotional embrace and kisses. The father orders the servants: "Quick! Bring the best robe and put it on him. Put a ring on his finger and sandals on his feet" (Luke 15:22). The transformation begins. Love has the power to transform.

The best robe would be the father's own. Draped in it, the son shares the father's honor and prestige. The ring on his finger bears the authority of the father. And as the servants fit him with sandals, everyone can see the superior position he now holds within the father's home. He is restored from being deemed unworthy to now being called a son to being fully restored as a child in his father's house. He could have been accepted and cleaned up in a less dramatic way, but in these lavish gifts, Jesus is overstating the truth that the boy is not merely accepted and tolerated. Think of it. This wretched son, who insinuates a death wish on his dad, turns half of his father's wealth over to pagans, degrades himself with pigs, and then returns home to find food and love. From this welcoming act, his entire being is transformed into an object of love, honor, and trust.

But did the prodigal change on the inside? Was his character transformed along with his countenance? Jesus leaves this question to our imaginations. This story is really about our heavenly Father, so imagine yourself at the lowest point in your life, maybe following your worst moral failure or humiliation. Tentatively you turn to God and look up. There He is in a dead run heading straight for you. He's laughing. He's crying. He's calling your name.

Would you change? Over the past fifty years of pastoral and missionary work, I have seen most people change when they realize God's passion and love for them. The poet William Cowper put it like this:

"To see the law by Christ fulfilled,
And hear the pardoning voice,
Changes a slave into a child
And duty into choice."

The realization that you are not just tolerated but actually the object of your Father's affection would surely liberate you. You thought there was a gap between you and God that you had to fix. Why doesn't He slow down and let you explain? You cannot experience this kind of love and not be affected by it. Who doesn't want this? Wasn't St. Augustine right when he said, "Thou hast made us for Thyself and our hearts are restless till they find rest in Thee?"

I know I am restless and long for a deeper experience of the Father's felt love. But I have always thought that I experienced little of it. Yesterday I had lunch with my friend Eddie. He spoke on and on about how he so often experiences the felt presence of the Father's love. One of his favorite Bible verses is

Galatians 4:6. "Because you are sons [and daughters], God sent the Spirit of his Son into our hearts, the Spirit who calls out, 'Abba, Father.'" He claims to know that Abba cry and experiences it often. I hadn't had his experience, so I was skeptical.

Driving home, I reflected on how so much of what I believe and teach about the Father's love comes from long hours of study and theological reflection, not the direct experiences Eddie spoke of. Then in my mind I heard this. *Do you truly believe that your diligent study and pursuit of Me was your idea? I have been working in you all along. You have always experienced My presence.*

You, too, might believe you are missing out. Perhaps it seems the felt affection and affirmation of the Father is still out of reach. It isn't. Otherwise, why are you reading this book?

FOUR

Elder Brothers

THE prodigal's journey has traditionally been the focus of this parable. Rejection of father and home and degradation in the far country is high drama, and the father's response is one of the most powerful and compelling pictures of the good news found anywhere. However, the prodigal's saga is not the point of the story. Many scholars, in fact, agree that it is not the main theme.

We see it in the larger context. "Now the tax collectors and sinners were all gathering around to hear Jesus. But the Pharisees and the teachers of the law muttered, 'This man welcomes sinners and eats with them'" (Luke 15:1–2). You see, the sinners and prodigals are already reconciled and sitting down to share table fellowship with Jesus, and the elder brother Pharisees and teachers of the law are upset about it and stand aloof. Jesus is talking about their refusal to come home on God's terms and telling them how and why they are rebelling against Him.

The pharisaical elder brother's central role in the parable becomes evident also when we consider the three "lost parables" together. In the first story, there is one lost sheep in a hundred. Then one lost coin in ten. One lost son in two. And finally, at the climax, there is one lost son refusing to come home. Progressively—mechanically even—the search is narrowed down to one moralistic good churchgoer who represents the religious elite Jesus is actually trying to reach. They are the ones who have yet to taste the Father's grace. Since they believe they have earned God's favor, they have no need for grace. Yet they are insecure, hostile, and defensive. This is a sure sign they are anxious and not at peace. They are the ones who have never experienced the rest, assurance, and freedom of their true home. Jesus maneuvers His listeners past the exploits of the prodigal and into a scenario that not only exposes the religious elder brother's problem, but also reveals the solution to it. So brilliant. Whatever else you believe about Jesus, this story, as well as His others, show that He is the smartest Man who ever lived.

What is the elder brother's problem? It is really twofold. First, he is preoccupied with his own moral goodness: "All these years I've been slaving for you" (v. 29). Second, he believes that because of his achievements, he has earned benefits and is upset because he has yet to receive them: "You never gave me even a young goat so I could celebrate with my friends" (v. 29). That is to say, he has fulfilled certain obligations and now demands payment. I call this contract religion, and we will discuss it later in this chapter.

Preoccupation with Morality

The elder brother does not come home to his place of honor because of his moralistic mindset. He compares himself and judges that he is better and more deserving than his younger brother who has squandered the family's wealth "with prostitutes" (v. 30). This emphasis on relative morality was a stumbling block to religious people then, just as it is now. This is the dualism we will consider in chapter 6. Acutely aware of how a focus on morals blinds us to the Father's grace, Jesus is forever trying to redirect us. Over and over, He explains that our own goodness can never give us right standing with God. Acceptance and assurance are already ours because of the Father, not us.

One of the most interesting juxtapositions in the New Testament is found in John 3 and 4. Jesus welcomes home the pious and orthodox Nicodemus in chapter 3, then befriends with warm fellowship the disreputable, unorthodox, and socially unacceptable Samaritan woman in chapter 4. He simply does not count right or wrong belief, or morality or immorality for or against us. If you are inclined to keep score of your moral achievements and failures, just know God isn't interested.

In addition to telling us that good and bad people are equally welcome, Jesus often shows how people who think themselves good are less likely to accept His invitation. One of the stories He tells that illustrates the danger of trusting in our own morality is the tale of the Pharisee and tax collector at public worship in Luke 18:9–14. It begins with a moral and religious man and an immoral and irreligious man going to church. The surprise is that the rule-breaking sinner is justified while the rule-keeping Pharisee is not. How did that happen? What did the good Pharisee do wrong? Didn't he tell the truth about his superior moral performance? "God, I thank you that I am not like other people—robbers, evildoers, adulterers—or even like this tax collector. I fast twice a week and give a tenth of all I get" (vv. 11–12). Yes, he's an upstanding man, but his attitude is exactly the same as the elder brother when he compares himself to the prodigal. Reliance on moral excellence leaves the good Pharisee unjustified as he exits the church. And just like the elder brother, he misses out on the freedom and joy of his true home. Those who think they are just fine are moving away from God. "The LORD . . . looks kindly on the lowly; though lofty, he sees them from afar" (Psalm 138:6).

What did the tax collector do right? He, too, told the

truth, but with one addition. He confessed his failing when he said, "God, have mercy on me, a sinner." To which Jesus concluded, "I tell you that this man, rather than the other, went home justified before God" (Luke 18:13–14). Even as he speaks, the tax collector finds his way home because he relies on the Father's character. Acceptance is always based on his mercy and grace.

The critical difference is that one asks for a gift, and the other claims a right. Our choosing to receive grace rather than our ability to perform is what brings us home. Jesus tried to persuade religious leaders through parables, but in case there was any doubt, He flatly states, "Truly I tell you, the tax collectors and the prostitutes are entering the kingdom of God ahead of you" (Matthew 21:31). Note that He doesn't say instead of you.

Reading the Gospels, we see time and again that the religiously observant were offended by Jesus while the nonobservant were attracted to Him, and He to them. When Jesus meets with religiously moral people and a sexual outcast, He praises the outcast (Luke 7). He also favors racial outcasts over religious Jews (John 3–4), and a political outcast over the objections of the establishment (Luke 19). Jesus constantly attracted and welcomed the irreligious while offending the Bible-believing moralists. From what I see, our churches today, in the main, do not have this effect. The licentious and broken avoid our services. If our preaching and the practice of those who attend our meetings do not have the effect on people Jesus had, then what we say and do are not congruent with Him. For now, wonder why the outcasts connect with Jesus and the elder brothers and sisters do not. We will consider this troubling reality in a following chapter.

I recently presented some of the above reflections to a denominational convention I was invited to speak at. During the question-and-answer segment following my talk, some of the delegates said it sounded as though I was saying our sins are unimportant. I reminded them that Martin Luther used to say that if we were not on occasion accused of being soft on sin, we were not yet preaching the true Gospel. It was a flippant remark that made light of something I do, in fact, take seriously.

I am fully persuaded that the accelerating moral decay in Western culture, if left unchecked, will make life intolerable. I think Christians and Jews and Buddhists and clear-thinking people in general should vigorously promote private and institutional morality. I also believe that declining moral clarity in the church and a lack of practical holiness denies our identity and makes us irrelevant.

The lack of clarity on moral issues in the church prompted John White and me to write a book titled *Church Discipline That Heals.*[1] My assertions about the radical freeness of the Father's grace do not negate or even conflict with an equal concern for practical holiness and the necessity of being salt and light to our culture. The point here is that focusing on relative morality blinds us to the truth that good and bad people alike are utterly lost. As Paul asserts in Romans 3:11–12, "There is no one who understands; there is no one who seeks God. All have turned away . . . there is no one who does good, not even one." In the early 1900s, *The Times* of London posed the question, "What's wrong with the world?"

The Catholic philosopher G. K. Chesterton wrote a brief letter in response. "Dear Sirs: I am. Sincerely yours, G. K. Chesterton." Simply trying to keep religious rules cannot begin to address the seriousness of our condition. Religious performance may even act as a diversion.

Jesus says in John 17:3 that eternal life is knowing the Father and Jesus Christ whom He sent. It follows, then, that death would be not knowing the Father. Much of Western theology has emphasized the legal aspect of our reconciliation to God. Jesus died on the cross, in our place, to legally cover sin. But will believing this automatically enable us to know the

Father? This is a significant issue, and I will deal with it in a later chapter. Here is the point. Avoiding sins or even the legal covering of them does not address our problem. Managing sins better or believing they have been legally dealt with does not give life. Knowing or not knowing the Father is vital.

Focusing on moral or spiritual performance puts us in the hopeless condition of searching for a thief on the rooftop while he is in the act of clearing out the basement, or like taking an antacid for stomach cancer. If our primary goal is to become a nicer or better person, then a good case could be made for following Buddhism or becoming a Bahai. There are many socializing and moralizing methodologies that work as well as or better than Christianity seems to. There is only one door to life, however, and it is always open. It is the door to the Father's house, and we get in by walking through it, not by moral or religious performance.

I listen to a lot of sermons, and much of what I hear comes across as moral nagging. Sunday school materials often have the same slant. Using Jesus' stories as pint-size morality lessons, they all but come out and say God loves good little boys and girls and is cross with bad little boys and girls. And how often do we hear of notorious sinner celebrities coming to Jesus and cleaning up their moral acts? Now that they are good, we throw our arms around them, but where were we when they were lost in the far country? My theological library contains hundreds of books that exhort and instruct on sin management. But there are only a few (some I have written) that emphasize the radical grace Jesus taught and demon-strated.

I recently attended a fundraiser for a national Christian ministry that runs programs for high school students. During the course of the evening, ten students took the microphone to tell how this ministry kept them off drugs and away from sex. Only one of the students mentioned Jesus. Behavior modification probably isn't in the mission statement, but improving morality appeared to be a primary goal. I'm thankful for youth workers who steer kids away from bad behavior, but if kids learn that Christianity is primarily about being good, they will not be steered home to a Father who loves and accepts them whether they are good or bad.

The Western church's preoccupation with morality and its ugly offspring, legalism, is what Alister McGrath calls "the dark side of evangelicalism."[2] If we do not perceive this dark side of religion, our contemporaries certainly do. In my youth, I worked several years as a street evangelist. When I asked non-Christians what they thought of Jesus, virtually everyone said they thought He was okay, and most admired him. When asked what they thought of the church, their response was not so positive. They said, "I think church is where you go once you get straight." "I don't think I could ever go to church. I already feel bad about myself." "I think church is for those who want to live better lives." I have never talked to anyone outside the church, and few inside the church, for that matter, who see the church as a welcoming family that is safe to come home to without judgment or condemnation.

There are some at the other end of the spectrum who applaud the church's emphasis on morality. I am occasionally asked to speak at Lions or Rotary Club luncheons, and more than once I have heard, "Reverend, I'm not a churchgoer, but I'm glad there are folks like you out there helping our kids stay off drugs." When I explain my message—God loves and accepts drug-addicted and sex-crazed kids just the way they are —I get a blank stare and know I won't be invited back. Whether non-churchgoers have a negative or positive view of the essence of church, they agree on what they think our core agenda is: sin management and improving moral behavior.

It is unfortunate that much of current Western Christianity agrees with them. When the transformational nature of free grace is preached, church leaders often criticize the speaker for promoting cheap grace. I have often been so criticized.

Grace is, of course, neither cheap nor expensive precisely because it is free. I agree with theologian Alan Torrance, who said, "I have never once witnessed an instance of cheap grace. What I have seen is a misunderstanding of grace. I have never seen anyone who experienced true acceptance and assurance and then said, 'Good, now I want to go out and sin.'"[3] In fact, as we shall see later, grace is the enabling and motivating power to true holiness. Paul says, "For the grace of God has appeared that offers salvation to all people. It teaches us to say 'No' to ungodliness and worldly passions, and to live self-controlled, upright, and godly lives in this present age" (Titus 2:11–12).

Elder brother moralistic legalism is at best an outside-in program that prompts shallow behavior modification. Grace conflicts with mere morality in that it is an inside-out transformation. As I feel truly accepted, I am more likely to be good to others and risk living a bigger, more interesting life.

Contract Religion

The first obstacle to the elder brother's homecoming is his focus on and confidence in his own goodness. The second part of his problem is his belief that his superior goodness earns him status, rights, and benefits. This wrongheaded view of how he relates to his father is what I call contract religion. It is what gets him lost.

Religious contracts are based on the notion that if we believe right and do right, then we may expect God or the gods to bless us. The earliest recorded example of this is the ancient Near Eastern fertility cult in which participants offered sacrifices to the gods in exchange for fertile women, livestock, and fields.

Contracts in General

A good contract gives both parties a high degree of control. They assume that if certain conditions are met, then specified results are guaranteed. A well-designed contract causes each party to mirror the actions of the other. Both have conditions to meet. For example, I recently contracted with a tree trimmer to cut down some of my trees. We agreed on $800 as payment for his work. At the end of the first day, I paid him $400. When he completed the job the next day, I paid him the balance.

Formal or informal contracts organize most of our interactions with others. We learn at an early age that if we act in a certain way, then we can predict results. If you say, "Please," then mommy gives you a cookie. If you take out the trash, then dad hands over the allowance. On the other hand, if you refuse to obey, you get punished. If you stay out too late, you get grounded. And our most important relationships are built around significant contractual elements. While marriage vows promise "till death do us part," if one spouse commits adultery, then all bets are off. Friendships are informally but implicitly contractual. Each friend gives something to the relationship, but if one of them ceases to contribute over a long enough period of time, the friendship dissolves. In our earthly lives, reciprocity maintains relationships.

There is a universal instinct to relate to God contractually. Do any of these crisis-induced prayers sound familiar?

- "God, if you get me out of this mess, then I promise to be more disciplined in the future."
- "Dear Jesus, if you help me pass this exam, then I'll go back to church."
- "Oh Lord, if you keep my adultery hidden, then I promise to be a model spouse from now on."

No one has to teach us these prayers. They come spontaneously to our lips, especially during times of crisis, and reveal our eagerness to make deals with God. We do this whether consciously or unconsciously. I have negotiated said contracts myself.

It's 1955. I'm ten years old. My mother, siblings, and I live in a shack on the river bottom in California's Central Valley. Mom works as a secretary and takes care of the old man who owns the land. One of my jobs is to herd and milk his cows. The one I call The Black Cow excels in treachery. My prayer life begins the day I attempt to lead her, at the end of a long chain, to greener pastures and she bolts. My hand gets tangled in the chain and I am jerked off my feet. Flopping like a rag doll at the end of the chain, I hear myself cry out to God my first religious contract: "Get me out of this, God, and I will go to Sunday school for the rest of my life." No one teaches me this prayer. Out of the depths of my flailing frame, I discover I hope there is a God, and I want to make a deal.

It's 1967. Jesus converts me while I'm serving in the U.S. Army. This episode is discussed in my book, *The Divine Project: Live Your Best Story*. Dramatic internal changes occur as a result, but my congenital commitment to negotiating deals with God remains somewhat intact. Initially, I am trained to fight in Vietnam, but the Army decides to assign me to one of its athletic teams instead. I am groomed to compete in the 1968 Olympics to be held in Mexico City. My sport is Modern Pentathlon, which includes five events: equestrian, shooting, fencing, swimming, and running.

I qualify for the pre-Olympic competition. It is designed to give Olympic hopefuls experience in Mexico City's mile-high altitude. I do well in the first four events, winning two of them. Things change, though, on the day of the last event (the three-mile run) when I come down with dysentery and am barely able to finish.

A few weeks later, the official Olympic trials are held and because I am still weakened by the intestinal bug, I don't perform well enough to make it to the Olympics. What do I make of this? I blame the sickness, but I reason that if I were a better Christian, God would have healed me and enabled me to compete for my country.

No one teaches me the fine points of contract religion, yet my gut reaction is that I must not have kept up my end of the deal. Failing to fulfill some unknown condition, I am denied the reward.

The Ups and Downs of Contract Religion

Contract religion awards kudos when we perform well and denies them when we don't. When things go my way—as in my wife is happy, my ministry prospers, people say and write nice things about me—I think I must be doing something right. I have kept my end of the contract, so God is blessing me. On the other hand, if I get sick or fall into a depression or some other bad thing happens, I suspect I have somehow failed to fulfill my end of the deal. Something like this is what Job's friends accused him of.

This contract mentality not only comes naturally, it is also unfortunately reinforced by a variety of Christian teaching and writing. Go to a Christian bookstore and look at the "Do More, Try Harder" genre. There you will see books telling you what to do in order to guarantee success in your marriage, your child rearing, your devotional life, and your sex life. You can grow your church, enjoy quality friendships, get rich, find peace with God, and have your prayers answered just by following certain rules. That is keeping your side of the contract.

The late Scottish theologian, James Torrance, flatly stated, "Fully 90% of all sermons I hear are either exhortation or condemnation or both. Nothing new is revealed to us since we already know we should do better. Such sermons turn every text into a rule for life rather than a revelation of Jesus Christ and the grace of God."[4]

I'm not suggesting that exhortation is necessarily wrong or that practical wisdom isn't useful. I am saying that it is important where we focus and what we emphasize. If we see our relationship with the Father in contractual terms, then we become the elder brother and will deny ourselves the assurance and rest of our true home.

Both brothers related to their father in terms of contract. The younger said, "I will work for you if you feed me." The elder brother complained, "All these years I've been slaving for you . . . yet you never gave me even a young goat (Luke 15:29)." Essentially, he said, "I did my part, and You haven't done yours—not even a goat's worth." Foolish. He was making points with someone who was not keeping score.

Some years ago, I saw the elder brother in my mirror. He shows up when I have a complaint against God. I thought God was treating me unfairly and that I wasn't being adequately rewarded for my work. The ministry I led had declined in numbers and influence while some of my peers seemed to be flourishing. In my journal I wrote, "Father, exactly what does it take to succeed around here? What have I not done? Haven't I worked hard enough and prayed long enough? For years now I have been consistent in all these." Sounds a lot like, "All these years I have slaved for you," doesn't it? I understand the elder brother all too well.

I shared this self-pity with my good friend, the late John White, one afternoon as we met to pray. After listening to my complaint, he said, "I have a Bible verse for you, Ken. Isaiah 50:11 says, 'But now, all you who light fires and provide yourselves with flaming torches, go, walk in the light of your fires and of the torches you have set ablaze. This is what you shall receive from my hand: You will lie down in torment.'" He didn't have to explain it. If I insisted on justifying myself by making my own light and walking in the glow of my own performance, then my reward would be torment—which it was. If I continued to try to earn by hard work what was already mine, then I would join the elder son as he sulked within earshot of his brother's celebration. I have finally outgrown that and now accept my acceptance more fully.

The elder brother appears to be about his father's business, but Jesus says he is as lost as the prodigal. Are you sometimes disappointed with God when He fails to reward you as you think He should? This may be a sign that you have been attempting to relate to Him on the basis of an implicit contract. If left undiagnosed and untreated, the results could cause problems.

Jesus says in Matthew 7:22–23, "Many will say to me on that day, 'Lord, Lord, did we not prophecy in your name and in your name drive out demons and perform many miracles?'" Sounds a lot like, "All these years we have been slaving for you, keeping our end of the contract." The scripture continues with Jesus saying, "I will tell them plainly, 'I never knew you. Away from me, you evildoers'" Imagine this. Jesus does not tell notorious evildoers to get away, but rather He says I never knew you to good churchgoing, successful elder brothers. We know they believe in Jesus because they say, "Lord, Lord," and we see that they have been effectively doing His work by prophesying, driving out demons, and performing miracles in his name. What could Jesus be thinking? As it turns out, He does not reject them because of what they do but because of *why* they do what they do. They do not ask for mercy or they would receive it. Instead, they insist on justifying themselves on the basis of their works. They say, "We did the work, now pay up." There is only one way to know and be known by the Father, and that is by His mercy and grace alone. It is as open to them as it was to the elder brother, but just like him, they claim to have already, through their own effort, justified themselves, so there is no need for grace.

This is not to suggest that our works are unimportant or that we are not rewarded for them. Jesus assures us that "everyone who has left houses or brothers or sisters or father or mother or wife of children or fields for my sake will receive a hundred times as much" (Matthew 19:29). The Father's loving acceptance is not conditioned on merit. How and why we obey Him is, however, important to Him. So how do we obey God properly? In I Corinthians 13, Paul explains that love is the true motive and power to obey God aright. Love for God and others is the only way to know and live in sync with the Father, who is love. He makes this point in the negative by saying that we can prophecy, exercise great faith, and even care for the poor, but without love we gain nothing (vv. 2–3). Nothing!

The elder brother didn't slave for the father out of love; he did it for a payoff. Those whom Jesus meets "on that day" have not performed miracles out of love, but in order to justify themselves. If love is the only right motive for doing what we do, then how do we get it? Or rather, how do we get in sync with the Father's love for us? According to John, we love God and others because he first loved us (I John 4:10) and because of the Spirit he has given, "we rely" on that love (v. 16). This then gives us rest and peace. "This is how love is made complete among us so that we will have confidence on the day of judgment" (v. 17). It is not our works, no matter how good they may be, that justify us and give us confidence. It is receiving God's love, experiencing it, and allowing it to transform us that does the work. Our motivation—to do what we do out of love—results from knowing the Father, who is love.

Self-justification through moral or spiritual performance leads to arrogance, bitterness, and self-pity. But imagine what it would be like to know for certain that despite your moral and spiritual failings, you are nevertheless the delight of your Father's heart. Think of how your life would look and feel if you could spend zero time and energy trying to justify yourself or prove your worth to others.

Nevertheless, the elder brother's moralistic contract mentality resists it. God's grace is in conflict with all religious systems. These systems want the world's view of justice; the Father, instead, gives us an innocent Man nailed to a cross who freely pardons His tormentors. Religion wants respectability; the Father honors prodigals and prostitutes. Legalism wants payment for performance; the Father ushers moral losers to the front of the line. We simply cannot know the Father and find the life we long for if we try to relate to Him as someone He is not.

Christ As Elder Brother

It is disturbing to see the elder brother in the parable relate to the father he has lived with for so long and yet be so blind. The Pharisees and teachers of the law who were in the business of knowing God shared the same blindness and were so threatened by the Father Jesus reveals. We could easily become disheartened with such examples of elder brothers who should have known better, but Jesus does not leave us with their example. He gives us Himself.

As I listen to the elder brother complain and hear the father remind, "My son . . . you are always with me, and everything I have is yours" (Luke 15:31). I imagine Jesus rising from Jordan's baptismal waters and hear the Father's approval echo throughout the heavens: "You are my Son, whom I love" (Mark 1:11). We know from John 17:24 that the Father loved Jesus "before the creation of the world." Just like the elder brother, Jesus has always been with His Father. Matthew 28:18 is Jesus' claim that his father has given him "all authority in heaven and on earth." In other words, just like the elder brother, all that his father has is his. Jesus and the elder brother have the same Father, but how they relate to him, however, is radically different. Jesus is our model elder brother.

The father in the parable says everything he has belongs to the elder brother. That would include the robe, the ring, the sandals, and the fattened calf he has just mercifully handed over to the prodigal. The father's love dips into the elder son's resources and blesses the younger. Technically, then, it is the elder brother who pays for the prodigal's salvation and reconciliation, and he resents it. Jesus, by contrast, offers His resources to the Father's saving purposes and does so gladly. "For the joy set before him he endured the cross" (Hebrews 12:2). Salvation and reconciliation always cost someone something.

It may appear that the parable of the man who has two sons is about a softhearted, simple-minded father who naively and uncritically forgives and forgets. But restoration of the lost doesn't come cheap. Someone always pays. It is no coincidence that Jesus chose the robe, the ring, the sandals, and the celebration as symbols of redemption in His story. He is stripped of His robe and hangs naked on a cross so that we can be clothed in the Father's glory. His hands are pierced so that we can wear His ring. His feet are nailed so that we can have His sandals. He tastes vinegar so that we can enjoy the wine of the new covenant celebration. He cries, "My God, my God, why have you forsaken me?" (Mark 15:34) so that we can experience the Father's embrace and be welcomed home. "God sent his Son, born of a woman, born under the law, to redeem those under the law, that we might receive adoption to sonship" (Galatians 4:5). We are to remember that "Christ redeemed us from the curse of the law by becoming a curse for us" (Galatians 3:13).

Hope for All Elder Brothers

Do you remember why Jesus told this parable? He sought reconciliation with the elder brother Pharisees and invited them home into the fellowship He has with prodigals. But even more than that, He invited them to live up to their true calling as elder sons in the Father's family. Jesus shows them how to do this by welcoming sinners and eating with them. He is what their mission to the world should look like. From the beginning, Israel is referred to collectively as the Son of God (Exodus 4:22; Hosea 11:1). This Son of God has been with the Father always. Inherent in Israel's privileged elder sonship is a saving mission to the world: "All nations on earth will be blessed" (Genesis 22:18), called to function as good shepherds who take care of the flock, strengthen the weak, heal the sick, bind up the wounded, and bring back the strays and search for the lost (Ezekiel 34:2–5).

Paul says of them: "Theirs is the adoption to sonship, theirs the divine glory, the covenants, the receiving of the law, the temple worship and the promises. Theirs are the patriarchs, and from them is traced the human ancestry of the Messiah" (Romans 9:4–5). All that the Father has is theirs, and Jesus wants them to join Him in spending those resources on saving the lost. "Salvation is from the Jews" (John 4:22).

Every time I come to the end of this parable, I half expect to find one more line saying that the elder brother has been won over and joins the family's group hug. But Jesus crafts a cliffhanger. He leaves the elder brother standing outside boycotting the prodigal's welcome while the father expounds on the absolute necessity of the party. "But we had to celebrate and be glad, because this brother of yours was dead and is alive again; he was lost and is found" (Luke 15:32). If there was ever a cause for rejoicing, Jesus is saying *this is it*. How will the Pharisee elder brothers respond? The question is left open; will the religious leadership of Israel accept reconciliation on the

Father's terms and take up their mission as elder brother to creation?

According to Paul, they choose not to and stumbled against it (Romans 9:30–33), and we are left with what appears to be an unhappy ending to our parable. But is it really? Paul later points to a time when Israel will turn from their initial blindness and accept Jesus' invitation to come home and know the Father he knows and share in His work. "Israel has experienced a hardening in part until the full number of the Gentiles has come in, and in this way all Israel will be saved. . . . For God's gifts and his call are irrevocable" (Romans 11:25–26, 29).

Until the full number of Gentiles comes in, however, the story will continue. It is the church upon whom the mantle of elder brother now falls and along with it the challenge of writing the final chapter. The question remains the same, and only we can answer it: Will the elder brother and the church accept reconciliation on the Father's terms and join Jesus in His mission? In the next chapter we see that we may have misconceptions to correct first in order to do this properly.

What if . . . ? Imagine a different ending to the parable. What if the elder brother was of one mind and heart with his father? Imagine them standing side by side, looking up the road at the prodigal stumbling toward them. Now they are running to meet him. The elder brother is younger and fitter and reaches him first. He crashes into him, hugs him hard, and whispers in his ear, "It's about time, brother. Welcome home. The old man will be here in a few seconds. I'll head home now to begin preparations for your coming home cele-bration. Tonight, I will be your master of ceremonies."

FIVE

The Road Less Traveled

THE CROSS OF Christ is central to all Christian traditions. How Jesus saved the world by dying remains a mystery. Nevertheless, theologians in the past have tried to make sense of its mechanics. The explanations they offer are called theories of the atonement. The dominant theory today in the conservative Western church is called the penal substitution theory of the atonement.

I will explain its tenants and contrast it with who Jesus is and what He said about His Father in the parable we studied. What I see there is not consistent with the penal theory. Jesus and the New Testament will lead us down the road less traveled.

A Short History of the Many Atonement Theories

The earliest atonement theory is the ransom theory. It is rooted in the teachings of origin in the third century. Its premise is that Adam and Eve, the first representative humans, sold us out to the devil. God gave our first representatives dominion and authority over His creation (Genesis 1:28). God said they were to rule over it (v. 29). Their authority, however, was not independent of God. They had authority to rule because they were under God's sovereign authority. He backed them if they obeyed Him.

Think of it this way. A highway patrol officer can stop you for speeding and issue a ticket because the state backs him. He has authority because he is under a higher authority. If that same officer drives over a state line or crosses and international border, he no longer has authority and can't enforce the law.

Just so, as long as Adam and Eve remained under God's authority by obedience, He protected them and backed them. When Satan tempted them and they obeyed him, they forfeited God's protection and backing. As a result, they, and the world, came under the rule of the devil. As the ransom theory goes, God had to pay ransom to Satan to rescue his creation. The death of God's Son was the price of the ransom. The thought is that the death of Jesus settled a lawsuit between heaven and hell.

Another atonement theory is the moral influence theory, formulated by Augustine in the fourth century. Simply put, this theory holds that the life and death of Jesus gives us the supreme moral example that we must emulate. By offering up His life, Jesus demonstrated the sacrificial love we also must live. How well we do this determines our state after death. Good morals now will be important later.

In the twelfth century, Anselm of Canterbury constructed the satisfaction theory of atonement. The idea is that the death of Christ satisfied the justice of God. He said that our sin is an injustice to God and, therefore, restitution must be made.

Anselm's theory was in reaction to the then dominant ransom theory. He saw the obvious flaw. After all, he said, what does God owe Satan? Anselm's satisfaction theory says that by dying, Jesus atones for our injustices, therefore balancing the books, so to speak. In effect, this means that God paid God and so satisfied Himself. This theory introduces, for the first time, the idea that God is acted on and conditioned by the cross. That is, God's attitude toward us changed because of the death of His Son.

I think all atonement theories have problems. However, the Christus Victor theory makes the most sense. This theory has been in vogue off and on for much of church history, and a version of it is part of Eastern Orthodox theology today. According the Christus Victor theory, Jesus represents all humanity. As Paul said, he is the second Adam (1 Corinthians 15:21).

In His life, death, and resurrection, Jesus was victorious over sin and death. Since we are in Christ, His life is ours. His death is ours. And His resurrection is also ours.

The cross alone is all that matters to other atonement theories. The Christus Victor theory is comprehensive. Jesus' life and resurrection are included. By publicly raising his Son from death, God validated and vindicated all Jesus said and did. Therefore, his enemies were vanquished, allowing victory for Jesus and all humanity.

Before I return to the penal theory of atonement, I will offer thoughts on atonement theories in general. I always wondered how what Jesus did to save a fallen world could be boiled down to a formula. It cannot be fully understood, spelled out, or spied out. What the Son of God accomplished will not yield to, nor be enclosed by, human logic. Theological geniuses over the past two thousand years have tried and failed. The real atonement remains a mystery that only God fully understands. Rather than attempting to explain it, I think kneeling in worship is more appropriate.

We now turn to the penal substitution theory of atonement and why I don't like it. Much of European Protestantism first adapted the penal theory in the late 1500s. It remains prominent today in the West, which is why I am talking about it. It is the road most traveled.

The theologian credited with early development of the penal theory is John Calvin, who was born in 1509. His early academic training was in law. He left the Catholic Church around 1530. His theology was influenced primarily by Augustine. As Luther and others got the Reformation rolling, Calvin became the leader of the Church in Geneva in 1541. Calvin excelled as a polemic and was a tireless writer. He published commentaries on most of the books of the Bible. His most influential book is *Institutes of the Christian Religion*. He is the principal figure in developing the theological system today called Calvinism. Among its tenants are the absolute sovereignty of God, the predestination of the elect to salvation, and the eternal damnation for those not elect. As a lawyer, he wrote in legal and forensic terms. He had a keen sense of justice; therefore God must also endorse a justice system. In essence, the penal theory he developed says: we are bad, and God is mad, so someone must be punished.

It seems to me that Calvin's God is conflicted. On the one hand, God loves His elect and wants to forgive them, but He can't unless atonement is made for their sins. Calvin and the Reformers who followed reconciled God's justice with mercy through the death of Christ. Since sin must be punished, Jesus was punished for us. The substitution part of this theory is that Jesus was substituted for us, taking the beating we deserve.

I began my walk with Jesus down the road less traveled when I was twenty-one. My dramatic conversion happened as I was preparing as a soldier to fight in Vietnam. After the Holy Spirit invaded my inner space, I began reading the New Testament on my own. For two years I never attended church. I cover this episode in my book *Living Your Best Story*. Following my discharge from the Army in 1969, I attended university, where, for the first time, I befriended other Christians. One of them invited me to his church. It was the Sunday before Easter, so I went.

This was my first exposure to the penal theory of atonement. The title of the sermon was, "The First Good Friday."

During the initial part of his talk, the preacher explained how mad God is about our sin. Reaching the climax of his sermon, in a loud voice he said, "On that first Good Friday, God in heaven raised His mighty fist above the earth, ready to strike." Standing on the stage above the congregation, the preacher raised his own fist high to illustrate. Then he crashed it down on the pulpit. He whispered, "But on Jesus instead of us." This was one of the most popular preachers in one of the largest churches in the area. I shuddered then as I do now.

The basis of this theory is that forgiveness requires punishment first. After all, we don't like to think that God goes around forgiving everyone willy-nilly. But the father in Jesus' parable does just that. When his boy limps home, having wasted half the father's wealth, the father forgives and restores his son without recompense or even repentance. His boy has already punished himself. In the world God created, we are punished by our sins, not for them. The Father Jesus knows is unconditional, unilateral, sovereign love. He does what He pleases, and for nothing.

The parable we have studied was first told by Jesus in response to the criticism of him by the religious leaders. "The Pharisees and the teachers of the law muttered, 'This man welcomes sinners and eats with them'" (Luke 15:2). Jesus was welcoming to those they shunned. He tells a story that ends with them center stage. When the father welcomes home his prodigal, the Pharisaical elder brother is incensed. He may well have said, "My father welcomes this sinner and eats with him."

The penal theory reflects the religious perspective of Jesus' critics. Sinners can't just be welcomed and included unless certain conditions are first met. If God forgives and includes us unconditionally, does this suggest that He is not just and justified in how He relates to us? If our minds are clouded by our own all-too-human view of crime and the need for justice, we will miss the breath-taking way God actually does justice.

Following the unjust torture and execution of His Son, the

Father exacts definitive justice by raising Him from death. God didn't kill His Son. We did that. By resurrecting Jesus, God passed judgment on the Jewish and Roman systems of justice. By overturning the injustice of crucifixion God justifies by making things right and good. God's justice is giving life, not exacting punishment. God's justice means Jesus and humanity have a new beginning.

When we did our worst, God did His best. Our passing judgment on the Son of God reveals our values and character. Jesus is the ideal human being. The ideal is what we judge ourselves by. He is the pinnacle of human potential and confronts us with the fact that we do not live up to ours. Who can face that? So we screamed, "Away with this man" (Luke 23:18) and "Crucify him! Crucify him!" (v. 21)

We rejected and judged our own human ideal. This is the ultimate expression of self-hatred and God-hatred. God said, in effect, "You have done your worst to yourself and to Me. Your sin is now complete." When Jesus said from the cross, "Forgive them," (Luke 23:34) and "It is finished" (John 19:30). the Father agreed, and three days later He made it real. On that day he fired all the bookkeepers in heaven because love "keeps no record of wrongs" (1 Corinthians 13:5).

Now He knows us not as sinners because of what we did, but as sons and daughters because of what He did. No wonder it is called the good news. That said, there is no conflict between God's grace and His justice. We can now look at the penal theory's conflict between forgiveness and punishment. If recompense or restitution is required prior to forgiveness, as the penal theory holds, what do we make of Jesus commanding us to forgive seventy times seven (Matthew 8:22)? This means as often as needed, even if no one asks or makes restitution, we are to forgive. Does Jesus expect us to be more gracious than God? Apparently, Jesus doesn't want us carrying grudges. According to what He says about His Father, God doesn't want to carry a grudge for the sin of the world—

so He doesn't. His Son's last words we, "Father, forgive them (Luke 23:34)," and He did.

Forgiving our friends is done every day as a matter of course. Say you have wronged someone. How do you know they have forgiven you? The answer is by the way they treat you. If they are smiling and open, you know all is forgiven. According to the penal theory, recompense must proceed forgiveness, so everyday forgiveness between loving friends exceeds that of God's.

After Jesus was killed and resurrected, He reunited with his boys. "When the disciples were together, with the doors locked for fear of the Jewish leaders, Jesus came and stood among them" (John 20:19). What now? They had all deserted Him. The night before the crucifixion Peter denied even knowing Jesus three times. Now they were inside a locked room with Him. What would happen?

No doubt, to their relief, Jesus was warm and welcoming, saying, "'Peace be with you! As the Father has sent me, I am sending you.' And with that he breathed on them and said, "Receive the Holy Spirit" (John 20:21–22). The real shocker came when Jesus put Peter, the worst offender who denied him three times, in charge of his whole project (v. 17). At this meeting, Jesus asks Peter three times if he loves Him. Peter responds three times that he does. Jesus then says, "Feed my sheep" (John 21:17). Jesus cancels Peter's three-fold denial with his three-fold reinstatement.

The penal theory is premised on its view of God's holiness. God is holy, and no one disputes this. However, the character of His holiness and how we emulate it may differ. The Bible says we are to be holy as God is holy (1 Peter 1:16; Leviticus 11:44–45). The penal theory says God's holiness requires recompense prior to reconciliation. Does that mean the most holy Christians should be the slowest to forgive? Given the critical and intolerant spirit of some churches, the penal theory may be bearing fruit.

Penal substitution suggests that God's love and will are weaker than our attitudes or actions. As we saw from our parable, the father's love was stronger than either son's actions. His affection for them could not be altered by anything they did or didn't do. Any consequences they suffered came from their own choices and not by the father's hand. The father saw it all and acted in his own strength, his own justice, and invited them home. As I said, how atonement works is a mystery. What we do know is that God gives it freely, and we respond one way or another.

The cliffhanger at the end of a previous chapter left us wondering if the elder brother would accept reconciliation on the Father's terms and join Jesus in his mission. This must now be answered by each of us. Are we willing to exchange the theories we may have been taught for real relationship with the Father Jesus knows, on His terms—the only terms available? Before you answer, one more misconception flowing from the penal theory must be exposed. It is religious legalism.

SIX

Religious Legalism

WE MAY THINK that the legalist in Jesus' parable is the self-righteous, rule-keeping elder brother. Look closer. Both sons wanted to relate to their father by a legalistic contract. The elder believed he had earned rights because of his stellar performance. The younger came home wanting to exchange his work for food and shelter. The father rejected both of their deal-making attempts. The younger finally accepted a relationship on the father's terms, which were the only terms available.

Legalism Rooted in Dualism

Our tendency toward religious legalism is almost inevitable due to our dualistic habits of thinking. We have been viewing and assessing everything dualistically our entire lives. If you have an opinion on what or who is good or bad, that's dualism. Society cannot function unless there is significant agreement on these issues. That said, dualistic thinking is inevitable and often necessary. However, we should qualify our dualistic thinking when it comes to how we believe God relates to us.

Religion is fundamentally dualistic. It says God is holy

somewhere up there, and we are not holy somewhere down here. Therefore, religion sees a cosmic gap between God up and us down. Anxious about this, religion seeks to narrow that gap. Doing religion is how that gets done. That is, believing right and doing right. As one does this successfully, he climbs the virtue ladder and narrows the gap between God and himself. The problem is that when he reaches the top rung, he finds there is nothing and no one there. He discovers that no amount of believing and doing achieves union with God.

In the parable we studied, we saw the elder brother proudly climbing the virtue ladder while the prodigal hadn't even stepped on the first rung. It made no difference to the father. As it turns out, climbers and non-climbers are treated the same. There is no need for a ladder because there never was a gap. The father and his two sons were in union. They were always one family.

God's sovereign love and His Gospel of grace are difficult for some to accept. It seems too free, too easy, too good to be true. From what I can tell, some combination of pride and anxiety makes religious people want to earn what God gives freely. Performing to get what God gives freely is what I refer to here as religious legalism. Let's take a look.

Legalism

I didn't grow up in church, so I was never conditioned by its legalistic expectations and rules. In my late teens I had friends who told me what it was like at their churches. One friend referred to his church as hard-shell Baptist. The women and girls could not wear pants. They had to wear skirts or dresses with hems below the knees. He said opposite sex young people were not allowed to stand or sit close together because the space between them was for Jesus. It was our first year in college, and he was questioning the legalism of his church. He was even becoming a little cynical.

I had a girlfriend at the time who was raised Catholic. She had attended a Catholic school. Outwardly, she was devout. She went to Mass on Sundays and confession on Fridays. She felt guilty about some of the sexual stuff we did, but Catholic legalism had a solution: the confessional booth. I drove her to confession on Friday afternoons and waited in my car. She entered the church and emerged fifteen minutes later with a prescribed number of Hail Marys and Our Fathers to recite. She assured me (and herself) we would be covered for another week of guilt-generating activities.

The Mormons I know are good people, and I would like them as neighbors. We know about a few of their religious legalisms. Some might make sense; others clearly don't. For instance, they are to abstain from drinking coffee. Medical researchers now agree that people who drink a lot of coffee are healthier into old age and live longer. The main reason for these health benefits, according to studies, is the powerful antioxidants found in coffee. As it turns out, coffee is actually a health drink.

Those are just a few of the religious legalisms I learned about before I got involved with the church. Some of them are trivial. Others are designed to assuage guilt. Still others are physically unhealthy. In the main, however, as we will see, they are often needless, heavy loads.

In my late teens, I heard talk about religious legalism. As an adult and church leader, I witnessed a lot of it. I never subjected myself to it and if what I heard was true, I inflicted it on no one. I am, however, concerned about the damage it does, which is why I address it. If we take seriously what Jesus revealed about the character of God in the parable of the father and his two foolish sons, a lot of problems would be solved.

One of the first churches I served as pastor was a large, wealthy, conservative, evangelical congregation. Several of my seminary professors attended this church and persuaded the elders to hire me. After I was installed, one of the elders took me aside and informed me of a rule. He said that when a man stands in the pulpit to preach the Word of God, he must wear a suit and tie to show respect. Seeing it from his point of view this made sense. He was a prominent businessman, and so a suit and tie were part of the legalistic requirements of his profession. If he was to be respected, he needed to dress properly. Legalism isn't just for religion. Some form of it is found in most groups.

He said to be respected while preaching, I needed to look right. This meant we had a problem. I never do anything to gain respect. I simply expect it. I told him I never wear ties and I wouldn't start now. I didn't think I was being rebellious or stubborn, although I have those tendencies, and there was no principal I was upholding. I simply didn't (and don't) like wearing ties.

Others tried to reason with me. Most in the congregation didn't care. Others were amused. They thought my breaking mold was a good thing. So, it was a mixed review.

I went tie-less for the first eleven months at that church. Toward the end of the year, thirteen elders met one evening to decide whether to renew my contract. The following morning, one of the elders who supported me came to my office to deliver the news. The meeting had been heated and contentious. The board was divided into pro-Blue and anti-Blue factions. The two main issues were that I appointed women to leadership positions, which was against their tradition, and that I refused to wear a tie while preaching. The anti-Blue faction strongly objected to both. Finally, they took a vote. Six of the thirteen voted to keep me. Seven said no. In their system the majority ruled, and I was fired. When my friend who was part of the pro-Blue group gave me the verdict, I felt relief. I was not happy there but would not have left on my own.

The termination was good for me, but not the congregation. I was mostly liked, so the news of my leaving caused turmoil with the church. In some cases, there was marital strife because members supported me while their spouses did not. Some of the young people got angry, and a few even left the church. Violating what I regarded a trivial legalistic dress code caused all that mayhem.

So far, I have mentioned what I consider more or less trivial legalisms that, nonetheless, cause problems. Others are not so trivial and may cause serious injury to persons and groups. Religious legalism is premised on the notion that leaders and their rules have authority. Keeping the rules will make you okay, and not conforming will make you not okay. We all want to be okay, so leaders can use that impulse to get your time, energy, and money for their projects. In many cases, that is the point of it all.

This gets serious in churches that seek maximum control and religious cults. Say there is a religious leader whom you and everyone in your group respects. Say he is smart and a good talker, so you take him seriously. Then, say he convinces you that he knows the mind of God and tells you that you are wrong in some respects. This, then, puts him in the position to tell you how to get right.

That's all it takes. He can access your time, energy, money, and in some cases your sex life. This could have been his goal in the first place. Call it legalism, emotional manipulation, or spiritual abuse. When the authority of God gets mixed up with a strong leader or a set of rules, we have potential for big problems. I cover all this and more in my book, *Healing Spiritual Abuse.*

As I say in that book, the only cure for religious funny business is Jesus and his gospel of grace. Paul learned this from Jesus personally. Paul was sent from the high priest in Jerusalem with pockets full of arrest warrants. He was headed to Damascus to take into custody those who were followers of the Way, which was what early Christians were called. Jesus met him on the road and temporarily blinded him. Jesus sent him to one of his followers, Ananias, to get further instructions. He was struck blind, then he began to see.

Time passed and Paul began to understand that contrary to all the dualistic ways he was raised to believe, Gentiles were, in fact, accepted by God and included in His family along with Jews. When he preached to them, they received the Holy Spirit. God sent His Spirit into Gentiles just as they were. And by His Spirit, he performed miracles among them. It was evident then that God accepted them just as they were (Acts 15:12). It followed that Jewish law need not apply to them. His conclusion? "For there is no difference between Jew and Gentile—the same Lord is Lord of all" (Romans 10:12). Therefore, Gentile Christians could remain Gentile.

This was a problem for Jewish Christians in Jerusalem. They maintained that following the Jewish Messiah required following Jewish Law. I can understand their logic. Paul had been preaching to and converting Gentiles in Antioch for about ten years. This is when, "Certain people came down from Judea to Antioch and were teaching the believers: 'Unless you are circumcised, according to the custom taught by Moses, you cannot be saved.' This brought Paul and Barnabas into sharp dispute and debate with them" (Acts 15:1–2). This dispute and debate led to the counsel at Jerusalem where the issue of Gentiles and Jewish Law were hashed out.

James, the brother of Jesus, presided over the counsel. Paul and Barnabas recounted how uncircumcised Gentiles received the Spirit with signs and wonders resulting (Acts 15:12). Much heated discussion followed until James stood up and announced, "It is my judgment, therefore, that we should not make it difficult for Gentiles who are turning to God" (Acts 15:19). With that, Gentile Christians were set free from Jewish legalism in principle. (A "yes, but" follows. You can read it.)

Paul's radical view was that the fabric of the old order had been rent and a new order replaced it. The law that had separated people dualistically had dissolved. The distinctions that made Jews special and separate—the preeminent symbol being male circumcision—no longer meant anything. To demand that Gentiles submit to the knife would say that the death and resurrection of Jesus was inadequate to save them. Paul would have none of it.

The issue of Gentiles and Jewish Law took time to resolve. On another occasion, Paul met with Jewish Christian leaders regarding this. Circumcision was again the central issue, and Paul didn't budge. He recounts that occasion in Galatians 2:3, where he says, "Yet not even Titus, who was with me, was compelled to be circumcised, even though he was a Greek."

Some time ago, I led a conference in Northern Ireland. In one of my talks, I referred to Galatians 2:3 as a turning point in our freedom from legalism. I said we hang Bible verses on the walls of our homes and churches, but you will never see Galatians 2:3 so displayed, though it is one of the most important verses in the New Testament.

The following morning, I opened my apartment door to find a small, beautifully framed embroidered piece that read, "Not even Titus was compelled to be circumcised even though he was a Greek. Galatians 2:3." That little piece of art hangs in my office. I treasure it because it reminds me how Jesus, Paul, and the early church, set us free from Jewish and all other forms of legalism.

Legalism in Community

Religious legalism, sometimes referred to as ritual, is universal and always has been. There is something compelling about the rules we make up or have inherited from ancestors. They calm our anxiety and seem to reassure us. Rules and rituals give our lives structure and the illusion of control. After all, this planet is dangerous, and who knows what or who lurks in the spirit world. Rules and rituals are attempts to mitigate against the unpredictability of life.

Major religions, such as Hinduism, conservative Judaism with its six hundred laws, and fundamentalist Islam, have countless rules and rituals. Some of these rules are unique to one group. Oddly enough, however, they have in common some important rules. The three religions mentioned above have detailed rules about food, sex, menstruation, and the handling of dead bodies.

Precise rule keeping and elaborate ritual are not, however, limited to major religions. I met a tribe of people in Brazil who practice their religion with specificity. They have a sophisticated dualistic cosmology dominated by good and evil spirits. They practice rituals designed to curry favor with the good spirits while avoiding the wrath of the bad ones. Just as with the major religions, these tribal people are very concerned about food, sex, and the handling of dead bodies. And just as with their more developed fellow religionists, men are not allowed to come into contact with menstruating women.

The similarities between cross-cultural religious legalism is interesting to me, but our focus here is church legalism. We may not be too concerned with food or menstruation, but we have many dos and don'ts that come from the same place for the same reasons. As with people everywhere, we seem to need rules and rituals to help us feel safe.

Jesus didn't give us a lot of rules. There is one that covers everything. " 'Love the Lord your God with all your heart.' . . . And the second is like it: 'Love your neighbor as yourself.' All the Law and Prophets hang on these two commandments" (Matthew 22:37, 39–40). This alone seems too vague and lacks the specificity the religious mind requires. We desire more rules, whether they make sense or not. Religious people need to know precisely where they stand with God and the community.

If we believe that keeping the rules makes God like us more, our relationships will be affected. We may think it's not enough for us to follow the rules; others must do so as well. This makes us a little neurotic and critical of others. When we don't keep all the rules (which we don't), we feel guilt and guilt makes us takes cover. Our faults must be hidden from those who have bought into the same toxic system. If we don't have gracious and understanding friends to discuss our problems with, we go outside our group, keeping therapists and counselors in business. I know because I am one of those people others confide in.

In this system, we not only judge ourselves, we pay attention to how others perform. We notice that they have faults too. Theirs may be as bad as ours or, hopefully, worse. This makes us feel a little better about ourselves and maybe a tiny bit self-righteous. The winners in this competitive environment are those who appear to be doing better or are more skilled at hiding. No one here is having a good time.

Religious legalism is about managing or hiding sin. This means we want to know the line that divides *okay* from *not okay*. We need to see how close we can get to that line and still be okay.

If the Bible or the rules are not explicit about something we want, what should we do? After all, there is so much ambiguity and many gray areas in real life. We pray. But we cannot see God's body language or facial expression, and He is not speaking loud enough, or maybe we are just not really listening. Depending on our issue, we may still be left wondering.

For what it's worth, I have adopted my own general set of rules. These are: enjoy life as much as possible, tell the truth, do the good I can, and never hurt anyone.

In a legalistic environment, with so much undercover happenings, we need information about others, so we gossip. Gossip gets a bad rap, but gossip itself is neither good nor bad. It depends on motive. We discuss people when they are not present. This is natural, necessary, and inevitable. Good gossip promotes group bonding and strengthens relationships. If a gossiper always tells you good information about others, you may think they are saying good things about you also. You feel safe with that person. There is more trust. If you have a problem, you are more likely to disclose it to them in hope of getting help.

On the other hand, in a competitive, legalistic environment, gossip is weaponized. If a person is eager to tell you bad things about another, and you believe it, that other person is diminished in your view. And since the gossiper is ready to spread dirt about others, you may assume they will do that to you. Now you are cautious and guarded around that person. If you have a problem, you will not disclose to them, ever. Again, therapists and counselors outside the group stay busy.

A negative gossiper earns a reputation and becomes less trusted and more isolated. The gossiper suffers along with the morale of the group. Paul addressed negative gossipers in Romans 1. They are, "full of envy, murder, strife, deceit, and malice. They are gossips, slanderers" (vv. 29–30).

As I said, gossip itself is neither good nor bad. It depends. Paul condemns bad gossip and then gives us the motivation for good gossip in 1 Corinthians 13. The motive being love. "Love is patient, love is kind. It does not envy. . . . It is not self-seeking, it is not easily angered, it keeps no record of wrongs. . . . It always protects" (vv. 4–5, 7). If enough of us took this seriously, bad gossip would not exist. That said, self-examination and concern for the spiritual and moral health of others is necessary if we are to mature. The right kind of talk and active involvement with others helps all of us to grow up.

If our attitudes and actions are not right, our friends should tell us, and we should help them in the same way. If love and grace is our core orientation, we can give and receive correction without a legalistic spirit and build communities that make sense.

Grace and Truth

John tells us in the first chapter of his gospel that God became our flesh in Jesus. He said, "We have seen his glory, the glory of the one and only Son, who came from the Father, full of grace and truth" (v. 14). Jesus was not a balance of grace and truth but the full embodiment of both. Some conservative groups emphasize what they see as truth. They say the Word of God says or the Bible says . . . fill in the blank. But we may be crushed by truth if there is no grace. Other, more liberal groups say it's okay to do your own thing. No judgment here. But we will never grow up if not confronted with truth. Grace is experienced best when truth is most clear. If we are forgiven, we should know why we need it.

In John 8, it states, "The teachers of the law and Pharisees brought a woman caught in adultery. They made her stand before the group and said to Jesus, 'Teacher, this woman was caught in the act of adultery. In the Law Moses commanded us to stone such women. Now what do you say?' 'Let any one of you who is without sin be the first to throw a stone at her.' Jesus straightened up and asked her, 'Woman, where are they? Has no one condemned you?' 'No one, sir,' she said. 'Then neither do I condemn you,' Jesus declared. 'Now go and leave your life of sin'" (vv. 3–5, 7, 10–11). This is grace and truth. With Jesus as our teacher, and the enabling of the Spirit, we wade into the messiness of life and speak the truth to one another in love. In so doing, we may become who we were intended to be and create Christian communities that make sense.

If we wish to live in communities where grace and truth come in equal measure, we must be clear about the God we envision. Legalism thrives in groups where God is seen as critical, judgmental, and punitive. On the other hand, if we see God as the Father Jesus showed us in his parable, legalism is less likely.

Religion is supposed to answer big questions. Where did we come from? Why are we here? What should we do? As Christians, we find a God who answers these questions in the New Testament. In Ephesians 1, we see that God had us in mind and chose us to be His before He created the world. God didn't make us because He was bored or lonely. God has ever been a relationship of Father, Son, and Spirit. The reason for creation flows from the heart of a well-adjusted family, which is determined to share life with us. We are not the result of creation, but the reason for it.

How were we included in this family? We were secured by God as His children by adoption through Jesus (Ephesians 1). Jesus came from the Father and took on flesh, becoming one of us. He reached us at our level. He entered fully into our human experience and descended to the depths of our nature. Hebrews 2:18 says that Jesus was tempted in all the ways we are. He stepped out of eternity and became a real human being. He united God above with us below. He is the mediator where God and humanity meet to share life. Dualistic religion and legalism die here.

Christian evangelists and other sincere believers tell us we must ask Jesus into our lives in order to be saved. I admire their enthusiasm and dedication. However, neither their words nor the idea is found in Scripture. What we do find is that Jesus has already included us in His life.

John affirms this from a cosmic perspective, saying that all things were created through the agency of Christ. "Through him all things were made; without him nothing was made that has been made. In him was life, and that life was the light of all mankind" (John 1:3–4). To the same effect, Paul writes, "For in him all things were created. . . . In him all things hold together" (Colossians 1:16,17). The all things He holds together includes us. We are in union with God rather than dualistically separated.

Jesus makes this personal. The night before He died, He

told his friends, "Because I live, you also will live. On that day you will realize that I am in my Father, and you are in me, and I am in you" (John 14:19–20). What will church actually look and feel like when we realize we are already safely home?

Religious groups reflect the character of the God they think they believe in. Jesus gives us a beautiful picture of His Father in the parable we have studied. We now consider what God looked and acted like as He moved around among us. He came across as sunny, serious, smart, shrewd, fearless, and powerful. He spoke with authority and healed the sick. Hundreds and thousands were drawn to Him. Crowd control was a problem when He was around.

People who were nothing like Him liked Him. And He liked them. I might believe God loves me in the abstract, but does God really like me? Jesus answers affirmatively. Yes, God really does like me and you. Remember that the crowds did not know Him as the visible image of God. All they saw was a beautiful man who spoke and acted with unprecedented authority and power. This fascinated many, bewildered some, and frightened and angered others.

On the one hand, Jesus showed respect for the Hebrew Scriptures, which he had memorized from youth. At the same time, He elevated Himself above them. Following are a few of the many examples.

"You have heard that it was said, 'Eye for eye, and tooth for tooth.' But I tell you, do not resist an evil person" (Matthew 5:38–39).

"You have heard that it was said, 'Love your neighbor and hate your enemy.' But I tell you, love your enemies and pray for those who persecute you" (Matthew 5:43–44).

"You have heard that it was said, 'You shall not commit adultery.' But I tell you that anyone who looks at a woman lustfully has already committed adultery with her in his heart" (Matthew 5:27–28).

He not only took authority over religious rules, but also

over our inner being. The new reality He inaugurates is not just external; it's also internal. If I take Him seriously, that makes me a serial adulterer. Self-righteousness is off the table for me. Daily repentance is on. Thank you, Jesus, for your grace and truth.

In Matthew 5:17, Jesus said he did not "come to abolish the Law or the Prophets . . . but to fulfill them." His point is clear. The old religion is provisional and partial. He has come to fulfill and complete it. Jesus is the new authority and now inaugurates the new reality. He called it the kingdom of God.

But words are one thing. How does the new actually replace the old in action? He and his friends harvested grain on the Sabbath. It was a violation against the old law. He healed the sick on the Sabbath, which was also against the law. He touched and healed lepers. This was illegal every day of the week. He not only spoke but acted as the new authority. More and much more. Wherever Jesus went, life blossomed. The sick were healed, the blind received sight, and those oppressed by evil spirits were set free. He plucked sons and daughters from their graves and reunited families.

He invited and welcomed the least, the lost, and the losers to dinner. He filled them with the best wine and food and there was. No doubt, there was even some dancing. These events were like the welcome home celebration the father threw for his prodigal son.

Jesus, as the real presence of God, left in His wake laughter, joy, and hope. When Jesus was in charge, everyone had a good time—except the uneasy monarchs, sleepless Roman officials, and dumbfounded legalistic religious leaders. He let them do their worst, knowing that even death could not extinguish the life He came to give. The life He came to give continued beyond His death and resurrection. Through followers like Paul and the early church, the life of Jesus spread throughout the world and changed cultures. Some changes

were dramatic and came quickly. Other changes arrived incre-
mentally and continue to do so. Let's see how this happened.

SEVEN

Moving Forward

TO THIS POINT, we have looked at the parable of the prodigal son from an inward and upward perspective: how we see ourselves and how we see God. Moving forward, we practice the insights learned. Deep theological thoughts are beautiful; living the truth Jesus revealed is more elegant. Living truth is worship that connects the resonance of heaven with the here and now. Jesus is once again made flesh in us.

The father in Jesus' story is anti-religious at every level of analysis. A religious father would condemn the immoral prodigal and reward the moralistic elder brother. Jesus' Father is first and foremost a family man. His core desire is to have His children home and at peace. No religion has ever envisioned God through the lens Jesus provides. By allowing His story to saturate our imaginations, the true nature of God comes into focus as it reshapes our own characters. We change in time, becoming agents for good in the world. The parable we studied is at one level diagnostic. We may identify with one or the other brother at various times in our lives. Well and good, but not where Jesus wants our focus.

All of Jesus' teachings, including this story, call us to

respond to the "big questions" I spoke of in the introduction to this book.

- Where did we come from?
- Why are we here?
- What should we do?

Philosophies, ancient and modern, psychological schools of thought, and all religions focus on this question: What should we do or how should we be in the world? Jesus answers this question.

We begin as the lost sheep, the lost coin, and the lost children. He calls us to become the seeking shepherd, the searching woman, and the running father. Our true identity is the third character in the parable, the father. Acting as He did is how we are to be in the world.

In the first chapters of Genesis, we find God hovering over chaos, brooding and then speaking creation into being. He then passes judgment by saying it is good, very good. God confronted chaos and transformed it into habitual order. Humans are unique among creatures in both nature and responsibility. We are representatives to creation, bearing God's likeness to maintain His order in His world. In whatever way we are God's unique representatives, we are to reveal His character in the various ways appropriate to each of us. This is what Jesus was all about and how we are to be in the world.

In the early verses of John 5, Jesus meets a thirty-eight-year-old cripple and heals him. Jesus asks the man, who has no idea who Jesus is, if he wants to be healed. The man answers a different question. He says he doesn't have the resources to heal himself. This sounds a bit like the younger son. Ignoring the man's doubt and ignorance, Jesus tells him to get up, pick up his bed, and go for a walk, which the man does. Miracle, goosebumps, happy tears, end of story—right? Not even a little!

Religious lawyers approached the healing in the legalistic way they would. They demanded to know why this cripple was carrying his bed on a rest day. What an odd response to something so beautiful. Who does this remind you of? Jesus responds to the lunacy of the religious mind by saying, "My Father is always at his work to this very day, and I too am working" (John 5:17). The Son does what His Father wants. As we follow Jesus, we do the same.

Examples from History

The early followers of Jesus, in the main, got what He was about and patterned themselves after Him. Church leaders today are well aware of the growing disinterest in their project. What they think is the Gospel isn't connecting with an increasingly secularized post-Christian culture.

Early Christians would see our so-called problems as laughable. They faced state-sponsored persecution, limited employment opportunities, exile, torture, and death. They were not only rejected by the Roman government, they were rejected by the Jewish community they grew up in. Yet they managed. Their world was not post-Christian. It was never-Christian, and they turned it upside down.

For the past two thousand years, many of Jesus' followers patterned their lives after Him, doing what they understood his Father was doing. As they did, the world transformed. The movement Jesus started became the single most transformative development in world history. For a comprehensive secular perspective on this, read the six-hundred-page *Dominion: How the Christian Revolution Remade the World* by Tom Holland.

The Christian Revolution upgraded moral and ethical assumptions, first in the West and more recently in East Asia and Africa. Today, the West is utterly saturated with Christian assumptions. Whether one is a believer or an atheist, each is judged by and judges oneself by Christian morality.

The Christian Revolution was unlike most others, which used political or military power. In fact, when institutions use force to impose Christianity, it proves counterproductive: for example, the Crusades, the Spanish Inquisition, and any abusive, controlling, religious leaders today.

The Jesus Revolution launched after His resurrection. His followers realized that not even death defeated Him or His mission. So they set out to fulfill His mission by sprinkling salt and shining light as the revolution progressed. Jesus foresaw this. "You are the salt of the earth" (Matthew 5:13), He said. "You are the light of the world" (v. 14). Not by force or coercion, but by the persuasive influence of salt and light, truth and grace. Over the centuries salt and light people, some prominent, most not, pressed on. Fishermen, farmers, slaves, day laborers, housewives, nurses, doctors, lawyers, CEOs, and even some politicians helped to radically improve the world we live in. And let's remind ourselves, the game is still afoot.

The Roots of Christian Revolution

Today we think of Christianity as a religion. When it arose in the first century, it was not a religion. It was a non-religion. A neighbor who was curious about a Christian's faith might ask where their temple was. The reply would be, "We don't have one."

Puzzled, the neighbor would want to know where the priests work. The Christian response: "You are looking at a priest, and I work wherever I find myself."

"But what about sacrifices? Where do you offer them to whatever god you worship?"

"We don't make sacrifices anymore. Our Lord, Jesus of Nazareth, was the sacrifice to end all sacrifices," the Christian would explain.

No one ever heard of something like this. What Christians said about spiritual reality didn't fit into any religious category then, and properly understood, it still doesn't. Contemporaries of early Christians called them atheists. As they understood religion, what else could they say?

From the beginning, Christians were subversive, refusing to identify with culture or homeland. They were happy to be viewed as alien, committed to a higher, transcendent reality. In a short period of time, they transformed their world—but not with armies or government coercion. What held the movement together and empowered it was faith in Jesus and bravely doing what He said to do, thus sharing the life He came to give. They were joyous and brave in doing so.

Many church leaders today complain about their lack of effectiveness in confronting our post-Christian cultures. Early followers of Jesus contended with a never-Christian world. Did they know something we don't? Did they emphasize what we minimize? Were they clear about issues we are vague about? Were they brave and we are not? These questions are worth pondering.

While not romanticizing the early church, we can learn from them. The early church grew rapidly and began revolutionizing Roman culture in the first two centuries. Historians puzzle over this. How did they do it? Why did this happen? How could a movement, inspired by an obscure executed criminal, come to exercise such transformative and enduring influence on the world that continues to this day?

Many are the reasons and there is a long list of why and how they accomplished what they did. The following examples may be instructive for us today.

Value of Life

The first and most important thing to note is that early Christians confronted a Greek and Roman culture that had little or no respect for the individual human being. If you were not needed, wanted, or useful, you could be shunted aside or killed.

Say you were captured alive during a battle with the Roman army. You might be killed or sold, depending on what was most convenient or profitable. If left alive, perhaps you would be sold to a broker for the Roman coliseum. He, in turn, could arrange for you to fight and die as a gladiator in the arena or, as a useless slave or Christian, torn apart by wild beasts. The coliseum was Rome's most popular variety show.

At the heart of Roman culture was naked brutality and utter disregard for human life. Showing mercy was weakness, which is why the Roman government nailed an innocent man to a cross and tortured Him to death. It was just another day at the office. But a few years after Jesus' resurrection, Christian influence penetrated Roman culture and put an end to coliseum spectacles, crucifixions, and much else.

We in the West assume that each individual is sovereign and possesses the rights and dignity equal to all others. This is the result of the Christian Revolution. The idea that individuals, regardless of race, sex, creed, or class, are equal under the law is found nowhere in pre-Christian history and remains absent today where the Gospel has yet to penetrate. What we call human rights is a Christian invention.

Disregard for human life was evident at every level of Roman culture. If you were not wanted, your life could be snuffed out. A father who wanted sons but got a baby daughter could dispose of her at the city dump with no qualms. The same for babies born with deformities. Early Christians were notorious for hanging out at garbage dumps rescuing throw-away babies. They took them home, adopted them, and raised them in the faith. Historians tell us that this was one reason the church grew so rapidly.

This very thing happens in some places today. I met Christians in Northern India who rescue abandoned infants that are left in the jungle for feral dogs to eat. The Christians must be stealthy. If they are caught saving a baby before the dogs get there, they are charged with kidnapping. Where the Gospel has yet to penetrate, unwanted babies are disposed of, even in sterile American clinics.

The early church introduced to the world the horror of spotting a naked newborn wiggling in rotting garbage. The church in India now models the heroism of beating away wild animals and facing criminal charges to save a child. The church in America is learning to fight for the unborn and the barely born while loving and caring for women who don't want to be mothers.

Many of us see the pro-life platform as a Christ-centered effort to protect the lives of the most vulnerable, which I agree with. But have we missed something Jesus wants us to see? How might the father in Jesus' parable respond?

Imagine how the story would read had Jesus told it about a scared younger sister, pregnant out of wedlock, and an older legalistic sister who would never let the younger live down her shame. Would the father have pulled his pregnant girl to him and said, "Everything I have is yours"? Is this how churches respond today?

The hardest aspect of the Father's nature to come to grips with is His utter indifference to other people's opinions. He had no interest in justifying Himself or winning arguments, He needed only to win His children back. Rather than focusing on the consequences of sin, which take care of themselves, we should care for the people Jesus did.

Race

I hesitate to talk about race in the West in general terms because there is nothing general about it. Differences and conflicts of race are unique to communities and individuals. What is done poorly in one place may be done with excellence in another. However, a snapshot of America tells us that all of the Father's children are not together at the party. If the church doesn't serve to heal and unify the family, others will come in and divide.

There will always be racist people, just as there will always be stupid people. We have our share of both. However, where Jesus, Paul, and the heritage of the early church holds sway, things get better for everyone. We should remember why this is, especially if we want to stay the course and keep improving. The opportunities and freedoms so many people find in America exist because America, in some ways and at times, edged closer to the values of the Father.

Racism was the norm in ancient Rome and everywhere else. Jesus set a different agenda. He welcomed and included any and all regardless of creed, class, race, or sex. Paul followed his lead in writing to his church in Galatia. "There is neither Jew nor Gentile, slave nor free, nor is there male and female, for you are all one in Christ Jesus" (Galatians 3:28). If this was taken seriously, racism wouldn't exist.

The early church listened to Paul. His churches were a mix of rich and poor, slave and free, male and female, Jew and Gentile. Women were leaders and, oddly enough, slaves became teachers. Imagine slaves instructing their masters in the faith.

In ancient Rome and everywhere else, slavery (often based on race) was universal and taken for granted. It exists today in parts of the Middle East, Africa, and China. Places where there is little or no Christian influence. Three hundred years ago that institution began to fall apart, first in England and its colonies, then in the Americas. The effort to rid us of it was spearheaded by Christian reformers, abolitionists, preachers, and politicians. The idea that no one has the right to own another person was a Christian idea. Progress came slowly, but it came.

On the first of January 1863, the US adopted the thirteenth amendment, freeing all slaves in America. Obviously, this was a great development, but it was only a start. Because we live in a consequential world, we are still paying for the sin of slavery. Race relations continue to improve decade over decade, but we have some way to go.

One of my sons, who is white, married a beautiful black woman—her parents are immigrants from West Africa. This would have been a scandal sixty years ago, even illegal in some states, but today it is an accepted cultural norm. Recent polling shows the vast majority of conservatives and liberals alike have no issues with their child marrying someone from a different ethnicity. That said, nearly half have significant issues with their child marrying someone from a different political ideology. How times have changed! What will change look like in the future?

The church, where it stayed true to the person of Jesus and the Gospel, helped advance racial justice. Where the church lost sight of the prodigal's father, it, in some cases, supported the evils of racism. The trend, however, continues upward. Things are better today for all races than in the past. Ben Shapiro is a historian and a public intellectual. He is an Orthodox Jew who rejects Christ as Messiah, yet lavishly praises Christianity. On November 7, 2019, he gave a speech at Stanford University, during which he remarked that American Christianity is the best thing to happen to civilization— ever. He emphasized that because of Christians, America is the freest and least racist country to ever exist.

We can celebrate the transformation of race relations in America and also look to the failures and injustices that still exist. We can hold two thoughts at the same time. The first is that the zip code and family you are born into have a far greater impact on your health, economics, academics, and treatment by the justice system than the color of your skin. The second is that black descendants of slaves in America are much more likely to be born in the wrong neighborhood and into a broken family. They face harder challenges than the average Caucasian, Asian, or recent African immigrant. What would the father in the parable do about this?

For years, the elder brother toiled away, seemingly without joy, doing the work he believed his father wanted done. Had he known his Father and been committed to the family business, he would have been in the far country bringing his brother home.

The Status of Women

In first-century Rome, when the early church began elevating women, their prospects were grim. Unless a woman was highborn or married to a government official, she was a mere commodity. In Rome and the rest of the ancient world, women were to behave while men did as they pleased. Fathers married off their daughters to whomever they wished. A daughter had no say in the matter. Female slaves and married women obeyed their masters and husbands without question. Women and girls were ruled by men.

As with everything else, the change for women started with Jesus. He smashed the mold of Roman and Jewish tradition. He welcomed women as friends and coworkers. Women traveled with Him and served alongside Him. At least one of them even carried the stigma of prostitution. There is no way to overstate the scandalous way Jesus related to women.

One of the most fascinating passages in the New Testament is the meeting Jesus had with the Samaritan woman at the well in John 4. Breaking all the rules, he approached her and asked for a drink of water. She said, "You are a Jew and I am a Samaritan woman. How can you ask me for a drink?" (v. 9). How indeed? Jewish men did not talk to unrelated women, and never Samaritans, let alone ask to drink out of a Samaritan's cup. All of this is beyond strange, but the most astonishing part of their interaction is that the Samaritan woman is the first person Jesus disclosed His true identity to. At the end of a confusing conversation, "The woman said, 'I know that Messiah (called Christ) is coming'" (v. 25).

"Then Jesus declared, 'I, the one speaking to you—I am he who speak to you am he'" (v. 26). Again, a Samaritan woman, who was married and divorced five times and now living with a man she was not married to, is the first person on the planet Jesus revealed His true identity to. Somebody say Amen! Jesus elevated the status of women, and the early Church followed His lead.

In Paul's churches, women were equal to men and some were even leaders. Paul sounded the death knell for racism, sexism, and human oppression when he wrote in Galatians, "There is neither Jew nor Gentile, neither slave nor free, nor is there male and female, for you are all one in Christ Jesus" (3:28). Neither male nor female . . . all one? If a husband didn't want to adopt the "all equal, all one" idea, he could find an Old Testament work-around. But in Ephesians 5 Paul says to both husbands and wives, "Submit to one another out of reverence to Christ" (v. 21). And then he says, "Husbands, love your wives, just as Christ loved the church and gave himself up for her" (v. 25). Mutual submission was shocking enough, but Paul tells husbands they must do more. "Husbands ought to love their wives as their own bodies. He who loves his wife loves himself" (v. 28). In the pantheon of feminist heroes, Paul should stand out.

Due to the influence of Jesus and Paul and the early church, women in Christian cultures are in most respects equal to men. In some cases, more than equal. Women in America today earn more advanced degrees than men. More are becoming doctors. The status of women has gradually risen since the early church got the ball rolling. Where the Gospel is not, such as in Muslim countries, women may be no better off than their first century sisters.

The Sick and Dying

Following Jesus and Paul, the early church believed that every individual is valued and should be treated as such. They demonstrated this dramatically during citywide plagues. When sickness broke out, those who could retreated to their country estates. There, they waited for the plague to run its course. Christians, however, stayed in the city to care for the sick and dying, often dying themselves. Historians tell us how their actions inspired others who joined them in their devotion to a God who actually cared about the suffering of the world. Caring for the sick and dying has always been a hallmark of the faith. The first hospitals in most countries were built and funded by Christian missionaries. We are the most persuasive when we don't simply talk about Jesus but act like Him too.

The Poor

Another hallmark of the Church is caring for the poor. Starting with Paul, who raised money from the Gentiles for the poor Jews in Jerusalem (1 Corinthians 16), the church has sought to help those in poverty. The Western church gives more money to help the poor than any other organization.

The church transformed the social and political Roman world in the first century. That transformation has continued. Where the Gospel is preached and practiced, life gets better for everyone.

Jesus, Yes

One of my early ministry adventures in the '70s was as a street preacher. I literally stood on a soap box and preached to crowds. I talked to a lot of people and got to know some of them well. I asked them about religion and Jesus. Many said they had either quit attending church or that it was never their thing. Why? To some it was boring and irrelevant—the longest hour of the week. To others, church was for people with an overactive consciousness, seeking moral teaching, or for those who wanted to clean up their act.

When I asked specifically about Jesus, everyone was positive. They all seemed to have a crush on Jesus. Church, no. Jesus, yes. I said earlier that Jesus comes across as sunny, smart, and welcoming. What if, after attending our services, visitors said that about us? People who were nothing like Jesus, liked Him. Why should that not be true of you, me, and our group?

I lived through and participated in two mini-revivals. One in the early '70s called the Jesus People Revolution. Hippies got off drugs and became evangelists and world shakers. Many of our Christian leaders today, including myself, got our start there. The second revival, in the mid '80s, is referred to by missiologists and historians as The Third Wave. The first wave was the Pentecostal revival in the early part of the twentieth century. The second was the Charismatic Renewal, which touched Roman Catholics and Protestants alike. It coincided with The Jesus People Revolution. I was a leader in the so-called Third Wave, which is associated with the Vineyard Movement.

During revival times, people spontaneously run to Jesus, and crowd control becomes a problem. Revivals are spectacular to live through. Who knows? We may live through another. What I want to see in the meantime is other Christians and me looking more like Jesus and His early followers.

We touched on a few of the ways Jesus and his followers made the world a better place to live. Jesus hasn't changed, and people are generally the same. We have the goods, so to speak, with a message and the Spirit who helps us. There is no reason we can't continue making progress.

The kingdom of God broke into history with Jesus. During the past two thousand years it has, by fits and starts, continued advancing. One day it will come in full. We began this book with the Father Jesus knows inviting everyone to a welcome home party. We ended chapter four with a cliffhanger. Will the elder brother church accept reconciliation on the Father's terms and join Jesus in His mission? We have studied some of the self-imposed doctrinal problems the church faces. We have seen the power of Jesus' work when it is fleshed out by his followers. There is no greater adventure, no higher calling than participating in Jesus' mission. It may be helpful to ask, if I were brave, what would I do? And then do it.

EIGHT

Final Thoughts on Home

IN HIS PARABLE AND ELSEWHERE, Jesus answers the "big questions" posed in the introduction to this book. Where did we come from? We came from the original, Trinitarian family. Why are we here? To be found by Jesus and begin our journey home. What should we do? Follow Jesus by doing what we think His Father wants done.

- Chapter one examines the extreme lengths to which we go that often appear irrational in order to support and protect family members.
- Chapter two witnesses the Father Jesus knows supporting and protecting his sons in ways that were irrational. A tale that comforts some and offends others.
- Chapter three sees the younger brother taking his father's wealth and running to the far country, where he loses it all through immorality. He wanders back home and is received with open arms and a celebration feast.
- Chapter four spotlights the moral elder brother

refusing to attend the prodigal's welcome home
party.

- Chapters five and six consider how bad theology
  and religious legalism distort the Christian family
  and undermines its mission.
- Chapter seven highlights the followers of Jesus,
  who radically transform the world by doing what
  His Father wants.
- In this final chapter, we end where we began:
  thinking about family and home.

Home Here

If we are paying attention, we see the powerful influence of
family and home everywhere. If someone comes from a home
where they don't fit, he or she will search for another. Thirty
years ago, I worked with gang members in an urban center.
The groups they formed were like families. Many came from
homes that were broken or their relatives were not safe to be
around, so the gang became their home. The gangs resembled
the way families are often organized. There was usually a leader
who maintained order and assigned roles to other members,
ranking them as elder or younger siblings. The leader was
essentially a father figure. A person accepted into the gang
automatically got brothers and sisters who had their back.

A close friend of mine committed a felony in her early
twenties. She was eventually arrested and sentenced to three
years in a woman's federal prison. She told me what it was like
locked up with hundreds of other females. Her story sheds
light on our need for family and home.

She noticed a fascinating phenomenon. Women formed
family groups. It seemed that they needed connection, a sense
of belonging, and protection from a world in total chaos. If
there was an established lesbian couple, some of the younger

women called them Daddy and Momma. The girls often referred to their siblings as brother or sister, depending on their masculine or feminine traits. Once included, the family had their backs. They watched out for each other as a family.

My friend was educated and had been a leader in the financial sector. She was powerful in her own right and didn't feel the need to join a prison family. Instead, she made friends with several groups offering counsel and entertainment. She was a singer who could perform favorite songs for each of the groups. She confessed that the confidence she displayed was a smoke screen. She was often scared witless. Not a Christian at the time, but looking back, she believes there was an unseen presence watching over her. Someone she didn't know had her back.

In 1972 I was arrested and imprisoned in Communist East Europe for Christian missionary work. I couldn't converse well with my fellow inmates because I didn't speak their language. I did, however, observe their social interactions. I witnessed what my friend saw in her women's prison. Groups gathered together and families formed. Unlike my friend, I was mostly at peace throughout my stay. I already knew and trusted the Unseen Real who had my back.

We may believe what Jesus says about our welcoming Father and sometimes feel His love in our hearts. Yet, we navigate a dangerous and chaotic world and get distracted. The felt love of the Father remains elusive. This will be so until we are in the presence of the original family we came from.

It may even be that you have caught glimpses of that face-to-face reality at certain points in your past. Was there a time and place where you felt totally loved? Was there a moment when you felt free to be yourself in a place where you fit?

I have a memory of such a time and place. When I was five years old, I lived with my grandparents and aunt on their farm, thirty miles south of Bemidji, Minnesota. I rose before dawn to help my grandfather milk his cows. Later in the day, I would help my grandmother churn butter, feed her chickens, and collect their eggs. At night, I lay in bed as my aunt read *The Iliad* and *The Odyssey* to me. I seemed to be the center of their attention and the object of their affection.

During the day when I wasn't supervised, I explored the forest that bordered our farm. The woods were a wonderland. I watched rabbits, squirrels, and weasels fight and play. I saw birds building nests and dive-bombing intruders, including me. I witnessed the cycle of life when a baby bird fell from its nest and was killed and eaten by a skunk. My adventure in the North Woods was heightened because bears and wolves roamed there. I never saw either, but I heard the wolves howling at night.

Sometime before the age of five, most children become conscious of and shy about their naked bodies. From then on, they cover themselves with clothes. I was slow to reach that point. Twice a week, my grandmother heated water and poured it into a wooden tub in the middle of her kitchen. I hopped in, soaked, and soaped as the adults prepared dinner. After Aunt Louise toweled me dry, I ran about the house naked and wrestled with Duke, the farm dog.

The first couple in the garden knew what that was like. I was surrounded by love, and so were they. I was safe and free to be myself, and so were they. I was naked and unashamed. They were naked before God and each other and unashamed. That's where we came from and to where we will return.

Twenty-five years later, I returned with my wife and new baby. We lived in southern Manitoba, close to the US border, not far from the farm of my memories. I wanted to go back to see what it would be like. Would any of the magic I remembered still remain? We drove into the yard where I learned to ride a horse, and I was disappointed. The cow barn lay in a heap. All the fences were down and the farmhouse, now abandoned, was in the last stages of decay. The woods that so excited and enthralled me seemed ordinary.

From time to time during our lives we may catch glimpses of the safe, loving home we long for. However, in our world, everything changes all the time. Good things don't last and, thankfully, bad things don't either. One day each of us will die. The good and the bad we experienced in life will die as well. My own death may come soon. What then? Will my quest for lasting love die when my brain waves flatline?

According to my atheist friend, the answer is yes. He believes that the universe somehow just happened and that we arose within it by accident. That our sole meaning in life is to pass our genes on to the next generation. I asked him if our thoughts and feelings arise from accidentally and randomly formed molecules, then why take them seriously? Wouldn't it be far beyond strange that a universe without meaning produced humans who are obsessed with finding their meaning? You take a big leap of faith to believe that. I take a leap of faith, too, but it is a much shorter leap.

I think little about my death and what follows because there is not much I can do about it. If my atheist friend is correct, then shortly after my last heartbeat, the lights will switch off, and then nothingness forever. If that is it, I won't be conscious to care, so it isn't a problem.

Home Hereafter

However, I do think a good and interesting reality of some kind awaits following the death of our bodies. I believe this not just because the Bible tells me so, but also because of how we are constituted. It seems to me that how we are made, and what motivates us, points to something beyond this life.

First of all, we are here, so something or someone made us. Think of what we know about makers and what they create. It may be a painting, a piece of furniture, this book, or something else. Each creation reflects aspects of its maker. The person who creates projects something of him or herself into the creation. What is made carries the imprint of its maker.

The question is, what or who is our maker? Following our discussion about creators and what they make, we can think back to our source. Consider how we are constituted, what we value, what motivates us. It is clear that we are hardwired for love. We are born with our love needs switched on, and those needs drive us. The need to love and be loved is a universal imprint. Since we are marked by this need, we may infer that our source is in some sense loving.

The apostle John says, "God is love" (1 John 4:16). If love made us, our need for it makes sense. The parable Jesus told is about a father who is a loving family man. He affirms what John said. Our need for love, family, and home are imprinted in us because our source is exactly that. If it is true that God is love, consider what it means. Love, as we understand it, is relational. The solitary deity of other monotheistic faiths is alone with no one to love until he creates something. The God who is love had someone to love from all eternity. Christians believe that Father, Son, and Spirit always loved each other as family. This dance of love, complete in itself, by nature, wanted to include and share. Love is like that. Out of love, for love, to participate in love, God made us.

In Genesis 1:26–27, God said, "Let us make mankind in our image, in our likeness. . . . Male and female he created them." Remember what we said about our Creator's image or imprint inside us? We came from the eternal Trinitarian family and bear its image. No wonder we want lasting love. We may find love and a good home here, but it won't last because death happens. What we long for is something unattainable here.

The seventeenth century French scientist and philosopher, Blaise Pascal, reflected on our dilemma. He wrote, in his classic work, *Pensées*, "What can this incessant craving, and this impotence of attainment mean, unless there was once a happiness belonging to man, of which only the faintest traces remain" (par 398).[1] This incessant craving includes our desire for love to last.

C. S. Lewis suggested that our need for lasting love and a good home is because we came from somewhere outside this world. In his book, *The Weight of Glory*, he wrote, "Our life-long nostalgia, our longing to be reunited with something in the universe from which we feel cut off, is no mere neurotic fancy, but the truest index of our real situation" (pp. 28-29).[2] If true, we are like the younger brother in exile, wanting to go home. The power and pull of family and home is real and for good reason.

I think Pascal and Lewis are onto something. Think of how we are born with our various needs and desires switched on. Then, consider that the world provides corresponding resources to meet those needs. The possibility of satisfying many of our desires exists. We become hungry, and food exists. We thirst, and the world produces lots of water. We need clothing and shelter, and we can have these. We have sexual desire, and (if we are fortunate) we may have this desire fulfilled.

We want love and a good home, and we want these to last, and they don't. We wonder why the earth provides for so many of our needs, yet some things we long for the most go unsatisfied. Has the universe played a trick? Or are Lewis and the Bible correct that while we were fitted for this world, we were destined for another? This seems to be the case.

Fifty-five years ago, in my early twenties, I was like the younger brother in exile. Unlike him, I didn't know I was lost, and I didn't care. I was okay with being a spiritual orphan. Then, unbidden, the Holy Spirit invaded my inner space, switched on the lights, and the scales fell from my eyes. Jesus found me and set me on my journey home.

Following this event, I began to take my life, and life in

general, more seriously. I asked myself one of the "big questions." What should I do with my life? Since I have limited time here, how can I best spend that time? It seemed to me that the most interesting and consequential way to spend my limited time was to follow Jesus, doing what I imagined His Father wanted done.

However imperfectly, I sought to do this. Consequentially, my time on earth has been more interesting, and I have seen more adventure than I would have otherwise. So far, so good. Over the years, I learned that what Jesus says about the world and myself is valid. It seems He knows what's going on in my life. Therefore, when it comes to issues that I'm unable to verify, such as what follows my death, I am inclined to believe Him.

Jesus tells us about the rest of our journey. "Do not let your hearts be troubled. . . . My Father's house has many rooms. . . . I am going there to prepare a place for you" (John 14:1–2). I don't know if Jesus is speaking metaphorically or, in some sense, literally. In any event, it sounds good. But, as I age and the words of Jesus sink deeper into my bones, I sometimes feel the approach of home. What I sense is misty and vague, of course, as Paul explains, "For now we see only a reflection as in a mirror; then we shall see face to face. Now I know in part; then I shall know fully" (1 Corinthians 13:12). And "No human mind has conceived the things God has prepared for those who love him" (1 Corinthians 2:9).

What has God prepared for those who love him? At the end of the book of Revelation, we catch a glimpse. In our life after life, at the end of history, we sit down at the wedding supper of the Lamb (chapter 19), along with all our brothers and sisters. Here we celebrate and worship the Lamb who was slain, resurrected, and now sits on the throne. Jesus foretold this scene in His parable. When the father's child returned home from exile, as we do, the celebration feast is on.

Celebration feasts are major social and sensual events where body and soul are nourished. Such celebrations are when our appetites for sight, smell, sound, touch, and taste are filled up. Along with eating and drinking, there will be laughing, hugging, singing, and dancing. Finally, I will learn to dance.

Jesus told us to rehearse for this feast by celebrating the Lord's Supper, or communion. This is not simply to remember His mission on earth, but also to look forward to a real feast. At the first Lord's Supper Jesus "took a cup, and when he had given thanks, he gave it to them, saying 'Drink from it, all of you. I tell you, I will not drink from this fruit of the vine from now on until that day when I drink it new with you, in my Father's kingdom" (Matthew 26:27–29). The feast He points to will be a family reunion such as we have never seen. He says that "many will come from east and west, and will take their places at the feast with Abraham, Isaac and Jacob in the kingdom of heaven" (Matthew 8:11).

Earlier I wondered if Jesus speaks metaphorically or in some sense literally. As we hear from Jesus, Paul, and whoever wrote the book of Revelation, our life after life will be physical in some way. If so, it fits with everything we know about Jesus. In John chapter one, we learn that Jesus, the Word, was instrumental in creating our world. After he made us and provided what we needed, "God saw all that he had made, and it was very good" (Genesis 1:31).

The Creator loves His material world. He denied us nothing that was good for us. "You are free to eat from any tree in the garden; but you must not eat from the tree of the knowledge of good and evil" (Genesis 2:16–17). The snake in the garden contradicted God, saying, "God knows that when you eat from it, your eyes will be opened, and you will be like God, knowing good and evil" (Genesis 3:5). We followed the snake's counsel, ate the forbidden fruit, and our eyes were indeed opened. We became conscious of our nakedness and vulnerability. The awareness of our vulnerability gave us knowledge of evil. We now understood how we could be hurt and, therefore, how we could hurt others.

Our nakedness and shame made us hide. It still does. God looked for us and found us. He explained the consequences of disobedience. Life now would be hard. Man and woman would suffer each in their own way (Genesis 3:16–19). Long after creation fell into history, Jesus came looking for us and began fixing what went wrong. During His life, He demonstrated His commitment to the physical world and to us by going about doing good. Those who met Him tasted his goodness (1 Peter 2:13). He proclaimed the Lord's order, the kingdom of God, in word and deed. He healed the sick, cast out demons, and fed the hungry. He raised sons and daughters from their graves, reuniting families, and much more. Jesus' miracles were not a violation of the natural order but the restoration of the natural order.

In John chapter two we see Jesus, his mother, and disciples at a wedding celebration. A celebration that was about to go badly because the wine ran out. Jesus' mother asked him to do something about it. Words to live by: when in trouble, call Jesus. Jesus then turned several large jars of water into wine. The Master of ceremonies said his wine was the best. Having the wine run out would have been a humiliation to the bride, the groom, and their families. Jesus cared about their embarrassment, and He wanted the festival joy to continue. John says this was Jesus' first miracle and a sign. A sign of who He is and the life He comes to give. At the wedding supper of the Lamb, we will see what he had in mind for us all along.

Jesus' commitment to and celebration of the material world launched the most materialistic of all the world's faiths. This suggests that our life following death will be material in some way. If so, we will not float on clouds playing harps, unless, perhaps, you always wanted to learn the harp but ran out of time. None of us live up to our true potential. What if we will have endless time to develop it, and maybe even exceed it? Who knows? In any event, such fantasies are better than looking forward to death, switching off the lights, followed by nothing forever.

During our short time on earth, we may lead interesting and meaningful lives. If exceptionally fortunate, we may find love, family, and a good home. If so, we should be profoundly grateful. Along with these good things, however, we suffer in countless ways. I have never met anyone who hasn't experienced tragedy or the malevolence of others. This is made worse as we see that the potential for malevolence is inside each of us. Our capacity to think or do evil is what Carl Jung calls our shadow. If we are at all self-aware, we see it. This realization alone is a kind of suffering. The thought that there is no end to it is intolerable.

Buddhism's first noble truth is states that life includes suffering. At the heart of Christian faith is a good man, wrongly executed on a Roman cross. Will there be justice? Will there be healing? In chapter five of this book, we saw that God's justice was fulfilled by the Father, through the Spirit, in resurrecting His Son. It will also be done when He resurrects us. The writer of Revelation tells us of a future when tragedy, malevolence, and suffering of every kind comes to an end. "God's dwelling place is now among the people, and he will dwell with them. He will wipe every tear from their eyes. There will be no more death or mourning or crying or pain, for the old order of things has passed away" (Revelation 21:3–4).

The theme throughout this book is home. William Shakespeare wrote that home is the most powerful word in the English language. The thought of home certainly exercises a powerful influence over our lives. The strong emotions surrounding it reveal our longing for a place where we love and are loved. A place where we fit. A place where we can be ourselves and find our true selves. Jesus left His home to bring us home. Even now, He is preparing a place for you.

To all prodigal sons and daughters and every elder brother and sister, *welcome home.*

About the Author

Ken Blue is the director of Good News to the Poor. The Good News is the message of grace, the charismatic dimension of ministry, principles of servant leadership, and healing of spiritual abuse. The Poor are the socioeconomically poor in poor nations and the spiritually poor in all nations. Before starting Good News to the Poor, Ken studied at Regent College and Fuller Seminary. He and his wife, Patti, pastored and planted churches in Canada and the US. They also built a strong family base that began with eight children and has grown to include in-laws, grandchildren, and even more children through spiritual adoption. Ken has authored numerous books, including, *Authority to Heal, Healing Spiritual Abuse, The Gospel Uncensored: How Only Grace Leads to Freedom*, and *Church Discipline That Heals: Putting Costly Love into Action*.

Notes

1. Welcome Home

1. Vicky Baker, "Celebrity Parents and the Bizarre 'Cheating Scandal,'" *BBC News*, March 15, 2019, https://www.bbc.com/news/world-us-canada-47585336.

2. The Father Jesus Knows

1. "The Story of the Quecreek Mine Miracle Rescue," Quecreek Mine Rescue Foundation, http://www.quecreekrescue.org/rescue.php.
2. C. S. Lewis, *Mere Christianity* (London Collins, 1961), 49.
3. See Ken Blue, *Authority to Heal* (Downers Grove: IVP, 1987), 74–78.
4. Ken Blue, *Authority to Heal* (Downers Grove: IVP, 1987), 74–78.
5. Walter Kasper, quoted in Clark Pinnock's *Most Moved Movers* (Grand Rapids: Baker Books, 2001), 6.
6. Dallas Willard, *The Divine Conspiracy* (San Francisco, Harper Collins, 1998), 244–245.

3. The Prodigal

1. Menachot 64, Sotah 49, Bava Kama 82.
2. Kenneth Bailey, *Finding the Lost* (St. Louis; Concordia, 1992), 127.
3. Karl Barth, *Church Dogmatics*, Vol. 3–4, trans. by AT Makey (Edinburgh: T&T Clark, 1961), 375.
4. F. C. Godet, *Commentary on Luke* (Grand Rapids: Dregel, 1987), 377.
5. Quoted in C. Fitzsimons Allison's *The Rise of Moralism* (Vancouver, Canada: Regent College Publishing; 2003), 151.
6. Kenneth Bailey, *Jacob and the Prodigal* (Downers Grove: IVP, 2003), 103–104.
7. C. S. Lewis, *Mere Christianity* (New York: Macmillan, 1952), 60.
8. Kenneth Bailey, *Poet and Peasant* (Grand Rapids: Eerdmans, 1976), 155.
9. Miraslav Volf, *Exclusion and Embrace* (Grand Rapids: Eerdmans, 1976), 155.

4. Elder Brothers

1. John White and Ken Blue, *Church Discipline That Heals* (Downers Grove, IVP, 1985).
2. Alister McGrath, quoted in Bruce Demorist's *Satisfy Your Soul* (Colorado Springs: Nave Press, 1999), 54.
3. Alan Torrance, lecture series at Regent College, Vancouver Canada. Summer 2002.
4. James B. Torrance, lecture series on Systematic Theology, Fuller Seminary, Pasadena, California, 1997.

8. Final Thoughts on Home

1. Blaise Pascal, *Pensées* (New York: E.P. Dutton, 1958), 398.
2. C. S. Lewis, *The Weight of Glory* (New York: Macmillan, 1949), 28-29.